STOP WHAT YOU'RE DOING AND READ THIS!

Carmen Callil is Australian, and has lived in London since 1960. She founded Virago in 1972 and was publisher of Chatto & Windus from 1982–1994. She is the author of *Bad Faith* and (with Colm Tóibín) of *The Modern Library: The 200 Best Novels in English since 1950*. In 1996 she chaired the Booker Prize and in 2011 was a judge for the Man Booker International Prize.

Nicholas Carr writes about technology, culture and economics. His most recent book, *The Shallows: What the Internet Is Doing to Our Brains*, is a 2011 Pulitzer Prize nominee and a *New York Times* bestseller. Nick is also the author of two other influential books, *The Big Switch: Rewiring the World, from Edison to Google* (2008) and *Does IT Matter?* (2004). His books have been translated into more than twenty languages.

Dr Jane Davis MBE is the Founder/Director of The Reader Organisation, a national charity bringing about a reading revolution b~ ~~~~~~~ it possible for people of all ~~~~~~~ ~~~~~ d abilities to enjoy ~~~~~~ ~~~~~~ l way. Their read-al~~~~

all parts of society, from rehabs to corporates to care homes, who might not otherwise read. www.thereader.org.uk

Mark Haddon is a novelist, poet and playwright. He is the author of *The Curious Incident of the Dog in the Night-time*. His latest novel, *The Red House*, will be published in 2012.

Blake Morrison is the author of two bestselling memoirs, *And When Did You Last See Your Father?* and *Things My Mother Never Told Me*, three novels (most recently the acclaimed *South of the River* and *The Last Weekend*), and a study of the Bulger case, *As If*. He is also a poet, critic, journalist and librettist. He teaches Creative Writing at Goldsmiths College, and lives in south London.

Tim Parks was born in Manchester in 1954, and moved permanently to Italy in 1980. Author of novels, non-fiction and essays, he has won the Somerset Maugham, Betty Trask and Llewellyn Rhys awards, and been shortlisted for the Man Booker Prize. His works include *Destiny, Europa, Dreams of Rivers and Seas, Italian Neighbours, An Italian Education, A Season with Verona* and *Teach Us to Sit Still*.

Michael Rosen was born in 1946 in North London. He is renowned for his work as a poet, performer, broadcaster and scriptwriter. He lectures and teaches in universities on children's literature, reading and writing. In 2007 he was appointed Children's Laureate, a role which he held until 2009.

Zadie Smith was born in north-west London in 1975, and continues to live in the area. Her first novel, *White Teeth*, was the winner of The Whitbread First Novel Award, The Guardian First Book Award, The James Tait Black Memorial Prize for Fiction, and The Commonwealth Writers' First Book Award. *On Beauty* was shortlisted for the Man Booker Prize, and won The Commonwealth Writers' Best Book Award and the Orange Prize for Fiction.

Jeanette Winterson OBE is the author of ten novels, including *Oranges Are Not the Only Fruit*, *The Passion*, and *Sexing the Cherry*, a book of short stories, *The World and Other Places*, a collection of essays, *Art Objects*, as well as many other works, including children's books, screenplays and journalism. Her latest book, *Why Be Happy When You Could Be Normal*, was published by Jonathan Cape in 2011.

Dr Maryanne Wolf is the Director of the Center for Reading and Language Research at Tufts University in the US, where she is an Associate Professor of Child Development. She is the author of *Proust and the Squid* and has published hundreds of articles on reading and learning disabilities.

Mirit Barzillai is a student of the written word. Her research includes investigations of the influence of semantic knowledge on fluent reading and comprehension. Her current work focuses on the implications of technological innovation on reading processes and interventions on both a local and global scale.

Stop What You're Doing and Read This!

CARMEN CALLIL · NICHOLAS CARR

JANE DAVIS · MARK HADDON

BLAKE MORRISON · TIM PARKS

MICHAEL ROSEN · ZADIE SMITH

JEANETTE WINTERSON

DR MARYANNE WOLF & DR MIRIT BARZILLAI

VINTAGE BOOKS
London

First published by Vintage 2011

2 4 6 8 10 9 7 5 3

Vintage
Random House, 20 Vauxhall Bridge Road,
London SW1V 2SA

www.vintage-books.co.uk

Addresses for companies within The Random House Group Limited can be
found at: www.randomhouse.co.uk/offices.htm

The Random House Group Limited Reg. No. 954009

A CIP catalogue record for this book
is available from the British Library

ISBN 9780099565949

The Random House Group Limited supports The Forest Stewardship Council
(FSC®), the leading international forest certification organisation. Our books
carrying the FSC label areprinted on FSC® certified paper. FSC is the only
forest certification scheme endorsed bythe leading environmental
organisations, including Greenpeace. Our paper procurement policy
can be found at www.randomhouse.co.uk/environment

Typeset by Palimpsest Book Production Limited, Falkirk, Stirlingshire
Printed and bound by CPI Group (UK) Ltd, Croydon, CR0 4YY

CONTENTS

FOREWORD

Why stop what you're doing to read this?

This year we learnt that there are many thousands of children across Britain who cannot read competently, that there are thousands who leave primary school unable to put together basic sentences. One in three teenagers reads only two books a year, or fewer, and one in six children rarely reads books outside of the classroom. Many parents do not read stories to their children, and many homes do not have books in them. Stories and poems, for these thousands of children, are not a source of enchantment or excitement. Books are associated with school, or worse – they are associated with acute feelings of shame and frustration.

The ten people who have contributed to this book are from very different backgrounds. Some grew up with a multitude and variety of wonderful books within their reach; some had parents who imparted to them a fierce desire for books and for learning; for others, books were hard to come by, or even illicit. But all ten are united here in a passionate belief in the distinctive and irreplaceable pleasures and powers of reading. They describe a poem as a lifeline, a compass, or literature as the holding place of human value. They each contend that books are not just for the classroom, but must be made easily available beyond it, because great books are essential to a richer quality of life.

These writers know that learning to read transformed their very brains, and that literature has helped them to express their questions and ideals, and moulded their imagination and sense of self.

This book is a manifesto. In a year of rude awakenings to low levels of literacy and a widespread apathy towards books and reading, this book demands an interruption. *Stop What You're Doing and Read.* Read these essays, because they aim to convince you to make reading part of your daily life. Read a novel because it will enable you to travel in time and space, or else quicken your sense of ordinary existence – family tensions, falling in or out of love, growing up or growing old. Read a poem, because it won't be as difficult as you think, and it might help you uncover and articulate a thought or a feeling previously buried deep. Read a story, if you're short on time, because it imposes a unique period of peace and concentration into your busy life. Read out loud, to your children, to a partner, because reading together casts a potent and intimate spell.

This book aims to start a conversation about the future. As the ways people read, what they read, where they buy their books and in what format are all changing rapidly, this book argues unapologetically for the paramount importance of books and reading in a fast-moving, dislocated, technology-obsessed world.

This book, like every book, is for you. Read on.

Vintage Books, 2011

Zadie Smith

Library Life

Sometimes people ask me if I am from a bookish family. I find it a difficult question to answer. One answer would be no, not in the traditional sense. My father left school at thirteen and my mother at sixteen. But another answer is: Christ, yes, they really were. Like a lot of working-class English people, in the Fifties and Sixties my father found his cultural life transformed by Allen Lane's Penguin paperback revolution. Now anyone could read Camus or D. H. Lawrence or Maupassant, for no more than the price of a pack of fags. So he bought these books and read them, and then spent the rest of his life boasting about all those books he'd read back in the Fifties and Sixties. I think he read to prove that his class had not succeeded in wholly defining him, and when he'd proved that, he stopped reading. My mother is a different story. When my father met my mother, his mildly aspirational reading met with the force of her determined autodidacticism. Pretty much the only place my parents' marriage could be considered a match made in heaven was on their bookshelves.

I grew up in a council estate off Willesden Lane, a small flat decorated with books. Hundreds of them on my father's makeshift shelves, procured almost entirely by my mother. I never stopped to wonder where she got them from, given the tightness of money generally – I just read them. A decade later we moved to a maisonette on Brondesbury Park and my mother filled the extra space with yet more books. Books everywhere, arranged in a certain pattern. Second-hand Penguin paperbacks together: green for crime, orange for posh, blue for difficult. Women's-press books together, Virago books together. Then several shelves of Open University books on social work, psychotherapy, feminist theory. Busy with my own studies, and oblivious in the way children are, I didn't notice that the three younger Smiths were not the only students in that flat. By the time I did, my mother had a degree. We were reading because our parents and teachers told us to. My mother was reading for her life.

About two-thirds of those books had a printed stamp on the inside cover, explaining their provenance: PROPERTY OF WILLESDEN LIBRARY. I hope I am not incriminating my family by saying that during the mid-Eighties it seemed as if the Smiths were trying to covertly move the entire contents of Willesden Green Library into their living room. We were chronic library users. I can remember playing a dull game with my brother called 'Libraries', in which we forced a crowd of soft toys to take out books from the 'library' that was our bedroom. Ben pretended to stamp them (they were of course already stamped) while I lectured some poor panda about late fees. In real life, when it came to fees, I was the worst offender. It was a happy day in our household when my mother spotted a sign pinned to a tree in the high road: WILLESDEN GREEN BOOK AMNESTY. The next day we filled two black bin-bags with books and dragged them down the road. Just in time: I was about to start my GCSEs.

I've spent a lot of time in libraries since then, but I remember the spring of 1990 as the most intense study period of my life, probably because it was the first. To go somewhere to study, because you have chosen to, with no adult looking over your shoulder and only other students for support and company – this was a new experience for me. I think it was a new experience for a lot of the kids in there. Until that now-or-never spring we had come to the library primarily for the café or the cinema, or to meet various love prospects of whom our immigrant parents would not approve, under the cover of that all-purpose, immigrant-parent-silencing sentence: I'M GOING TO THE LIBRARY. When the exams came, we stopped goofing off. There's no point in goofing off in a library: you're acutely aware that the only person's time you're wasting is your own. We sat next to each other at the long white tables and used the library computers and did not speak. Now we were reading for *our* lives. After my exams I felt I owed those students a collective debt – all those John Kelly girls and John Kelly boys, kids from Hampstead Comp, and Aylestone (as it was known then), from La Swap and William Ellis. We may not have spoken to each other, except to ask for sharpeners or paper, but by turning up we acted as each other's conscience. A reason to stay another hour, and another hour after that. It was a community of individuals, working to individual goals, in a public space. It's short-sighted to think all our goals were bookish ones. I happened to be in the library in the hope it would lead to me to other libraries, but my fellow students were seeking all kinds of futures: in dentistry, in social work, in education, in catering, in engineering, in management. We all learned a lot of things in Willesden Green Library, and we learned *how* to learn things, which is more important. I learned that 'Milton was of the devil's party without knowing it' and that the Brontës had a brother. I found out who Henry V was and what Malcolm X did. I came to understand why silence is necessary for serious study, and what the point of coffee is. I discovered that there exist people who write not just books, but books about books, and finding that out changed my life.

Still, it's important not to overly romanticise these things. Willesden Green Library was not to be confused with the British Library. Sometimes whole shelves of books would be missing, lost, depressingly defaced or torn. Sometimes people would come in just to have a conversation, while I bit my biros to pieces in frustration. Later I learned what a monumental and sacred thing a library can be. I have spent my adult life in libraries that make a local library like Willesden Green's, like Kensal Rise's, like Kilburn's, look very small indeed; to some people, clearly, quite small enough to be rid of, without much regret.

But I know I never would have seen a single university library if I had not grown up living a hundred yards from that library in Willesden Green. Local libraries are gateways – not only to other libraries, but to other lives. Of course I can see that if you went to Eton or Harrow or Winchester or Westminster – like so many of the present Cabinet – you might not understand the point of such lowly gateways, or be able to conceive why anyone would crawl on their hands and knees for the privilege of entering one. It has always been, and always will be, very difficult to explain to people with money what it means not to have money. If education matters to you, they ask, and if libraries matter to you, well, why wouldn't you be willing to pay for them if you value them? They are the kind of people who believe value can only be measured in money, at the extreme end of which logic lies the dangerous idea that people who do not generate a lot of money for their families cannot possibly value their families as people with money do.

My own family put a very high value on education, on bookishness, but it happened that they did not have the money to demonstrate this fact in a manner that the present government seems able to comprehend. Like many people without a lot of money, we relied on our public services. Not as a frippery, not as a pointless addition, not as an excuse for personal stagnation, but as a necessary gateway to better opportunities. Like millions of British people, we paid our taxes in the hope that they would be used to establish shared institutions from which all might benefit equally. We understood very well that there are people who have no need of these services, who really cannot see the point of them. Who have made their own private arrangements, in health-care and education and property and travel and lifestyle, and who have a private library in their own private houses. These days I also have a private library in my own private house. And I have a library in the university in which I teach. But if you've benefited from the use of shared institutions, you know that to abandon them once they are no longer a personal necessity is like Wile E. Coyote laying down a rope bridge between two precipices, only to blow it up once he's reached the other side – so that no one might follow him. Apart from anything else, you may not be as wily as you think you are. One day, you might find that back on the other side of that chasm is where you want to be. You might discover how quickly an afternoon with a toddler passes in a local library, quicker than practically anywhere else. You might urgently want to know something about your street in 1894. You might realise that giving up smoking or writing a novel is easier to do when you're one of a group of people all seated on some fold-up chairs in a circle. It might strike you that what you really want in life is silence. Despite the many wonders of the Internet, you might suddenly long for the smell of old books.

But even if none of these things apply to you, even if community is your idea of hell, the principle remains. Community exists in Britain, and no matter how many individuals opt out of it, the commons of British life will always be the greater force, practically and morally. Community is a partnership between government and the people, and it is depressing to hear the language of community – the so-called 'Big Society' – being used to disguise the low motives of one side of that partnership as it attempts to worm out of the deal. What could be better, they suggest, than handing people back the power so they might build their own schools, their own libraries? Better to leave people to the already onerous tasks of building their lives and paying their taxes. Leave the building of infrastructure to government, and the protection of public services to government – that being government's mandate, and the only possible justification for its power. That the grotesque losses of the private sector are to be nationalised, cut from our schools and our libraries, our social services and our health service – in short, from our national heritage – represents a policy so shameful I doubt this government will ever live it down. Perhaps it's because they know what the history books will make of them that our politicians are so cavalier with our libraries: from their point of view, the fewer places where you can find a history book these days, the better.

Blake Morrison

Twelve Thoughts About Reading

The Great Escape

A friend once told me how she'd built a wall of
books round her bed as a teenager. The books
came from the local library, and she piled them
up like bricks or breezeblocks to shut herself
off from her family. The image disturbed me:
books as a barrier, bed as a lonely prison cell, a
miserable girl immuring herself in words. But for
her the memory was a positive one. Those books
enclosed a space in which she felt safe and happy
– not a bleak dungeon, but a huge room thronging
with people who (unlike her family) made her feel
at home. Till then she hadn't known that other
world existed. And imaginary though it was – a
world invented by poets and novelists – it was as
real to her as the world from which she was

escaping. In fact, the books were less a wall than a ladder. By reading them, and learning from them, and then flourishing academically at school, she climbed up and away to freedom.

She went on to become a writer. But it's not only writers whose lives are transformed by books. And it's not only the young and miserable who use books to escape their circumstances. The story has stuck in my mind not because it's unusual, but because so many other people have similar stories to tell. To an extent it's even my own story: not that my childhood was unhappy, but the literature I began to discover round the age of sixteen – Joyce, Lawrence, Eliot, Hardy, Wilfred Owen – took my life in a new direction, one that I'd not expected or been encouraged to follow.

Perhaps my friend's story also struck home because I knew it already, from books. Here is David Copperfield, describing how he escaped from the oppressive regime imposed by the Murdstones:

> My father had left a small collection of
> books in a little room upstairs, to which I
> had access (for it adjoined my own) and
> which nobody else in our house ever
> troubled. From that blessed little room,

Roderick Random, Peregrine Pickle,
Humphrey Clinker, Tom Jones, the Vicar of
Wakefield, Don Quixote, Gil Blas and
Robinson Crusoe came out, a glorious host,
to keep me company. They kept alive my
fancy, and my hope of something beyond
that place and time – they, and the Arabian
Knights, and the Tales of the Genii – and
did me no harm; for whatever harm was in
some of them was not there for me.

A hope of something beyond our place and time.
This is what books – the best books – give us: a
lifeline, a reason to believe, a way to breathe
more freely.

Giving and taking

However much they give, books also demand
that we give something back. They may exist as
physical objects without ever being opened, but
they don't exist as texts until someone reads them.
What we bring to a book – our experiences, our
enthusiasms, our desire to know more – will affect
our reading as much as the words themselves. As
Alberto Manguel puts it, 'The existence of the
text is a silent existence, silent until the moment

in which a reader reads it. Only when the able eye makes contact with the markings on the tablet does the text come to active life. All writing depends on the generosity of the reader.'

Ownership

To begin with, while a book is being conceived, authors have exclusive rights over it. The book is their baby: it's they who bring it into being, nurture its development, see it through to maturity. But once it's out there in the world, the book has a life of its own: it slides away from its creator and becomes independent. Publication is a coming-of-age party and a handing-over. Authors may flinch and protest if what we take from their text differs from what they intended, but they have to let go. Their baby is ours now.

You can possess a book without really owning it, though. Beyond ownership in a commercial or legal sense, there's ownership of an emotional or metaphysical kind – when a book speaks so powerfully to us that we feel it's ours exclusively: that it exists just for us. People we meet sometimes have this effect too; they look into our eyes, and speak in a hushed, intimate voice, and make us feel we're uniquely important to them – before going on to do the same to someone else. In life, we call these people flirts. The best books are flirtatious, too, since they seem to be ours alone when in reality they're anyone's.

Illusory or not, a feeling of ownership is crucial to the enjoyment of a book, and many authors have described a moment in childhood or adolescence when they are so absorbed or 'taken over' by a text that the gap between it and them disappears. Take the writer Eva Hoffman, for example, born in Cracow in the era of Communism. In her memoir *Lost in Translation* she describes her disenchantment with the reading assigned to her at school – stern political stuff about collective farms and the dignity of labour. But when her mother starts taking her to the library, she comes across more exciting material – Jules Verne, Boccaccio, *Alice in Wonderland*, *Doctor Dolittle*, and *Anne of Green Gables*. The last makes a particularly deep impression: 'As long as I'm reading, I assume that I am this girl growing up on Prince Edward Island; the novel's words enter my head as if they were emanating from it. Since I experience what they describe so vividly, they must be mine.'

In her memoir *Bad Blood* Lorna Sage describes having the same feeling about poetry: 'I had hundreds and hundreds of lines of verse by heart, which I paraded past my mind's eye as though in a way they were mine.' And in her memoir *Once in a House on Fire* Andrea Ashworth similarly recalls how when she read Dylan Thomas's 'Do Not Go Gentle into that Good Night' she took it to be a poem not about death, but about her own condition: 'for me, the dying of the light had to do with being buried alive in your own smoky front room with your family, stuck together for ever and ever, in front of the TV'. For Ashworth, growing up under the tyranny of an abusive stepfather, books served an urgent purpose. Reading them in secret, in her bedroom, 'was like holding my breath underwater, immersing myself for as long as possible, until some yell or bang or even a burst of laughter broke in'. The texts she studied at school or borrowed from her posh friend Tamsyn – Hardy, T. S. Eliot, Larkin, Dickens, Charlotte and Emily Brontë – not only explained her sense of suffocation, but liberated her from it: 'They lifted you up, towards a sort of light, instead of dragging you down into darkness. And the excitement stayed with you, even carried on growing, after you closed the book.'

When a poem or story is working, we don't just identify with the persona or main protagonist, we *become* them. At an age when I should have known better I was so taken by Howard Kirk, the anti-hero of Malcolm Bradbury's *The History Man*, that I spent a couple of months behaving like him – in one case coming on to a girl at a party with a swagger that was his, not mine.

Ownership: an extreme case of appropriation.

Horace: *Mutato nomine, de te fabula narratur.*
'Change the name and the story is about you.'

Though ostensibly a novel, Tobias Wolff's *Old School* is strongly autobiographical and in effect makes up the centre panel between his memoirs *This Boy's Life* (about his peripatetic childhood) and *In Pharaoh's Army* (about his years in Vietnam). Its subject is his experience as a scholarship boy and sixth-former in an American private school. He is making his first efforts to write at this point, in a hothouse atmosphere where star pupils compete for prizes and appearances in the *Troubadour*, the school magazine. One day, despairing of how difficult it is to write with truth and authenticity, he comes across a story called 'Summer Dance', published in the magazine of a nearby girls' school, and is bowled over by it:

> I went back to the beginning and read it
> again, slowly this time, feeling all the while
> as if my inmost vault had been smashed
> open and looted and every hidden thing
> spread out across the pages. From the very
> first sentence I was looking myself right in
> the face . . . The whole thing came straight
> from the truthful diary I'd never kept.

Inspired, he sits down and rewrites 'Summer Dance' as if it were indeed his story, keeping the title, but changing the name of the narrator (a girl, Ruth) to his own: 'I didn't have a lot of adjusting to do. These thoughts were my thoughts, this life my own.' He feels as if he's giving himself away as never before, 'beyond all recall', but determinedly persists till the story is finished. He is pleased by the result, but shocked by how nakedly it has exposed him: 'Anyone who read this story would know who I was.'

His story is shortlisted for a school prize, and Ernest Hemingway – acting as judge – chooses it as the winner; he is scheduled to present the award to Wolff in person. But then someone notices the uncanny resemblance between the prizewinning story and the one published five years previously in the girls' school magazine. Summoned to the headmaster's office, Wolff is asked to explain himself. Which he can't. Even when a photocopy of the original story is handed to him, he's lost for words:

> I'd completely forgotten it. It had flown
> my mind as soon as I'd begun reading the
> story that night in the *Troubadour* office
> and seen my own life laid bare on the
> page, and in all the time since then I'd
> never thought of 'Summer Dance' as
> anyone's story but mine.
>
> And I still didn't; not really. Even with
> the proof in hand, even knowing that
> someone named Susan Friedman had written
> the story, I still thought of it as mine.

Found guilty of plagiarism and of bringing the school into disrepute, Wolff is expelled. Yet he commits his crime in all innocence. It's an extreme case of a common phenomenon: reading as ownership, reading as appropriation.

As Horace said, 'Change the name and the story is about you.'

Daring to say 'I'

In recent years I've gone back to teaching creative writing at Goldsmiths College, London, where for several years, in my twenties, I ran a workshop for poets. These days most of my students are life writers, working in prose. The demands of the two forms are very different. But the poets and life writers have something important in common: the use of the first-person pronoun. Speaking in one's own voice – 'daring to say I', as one student put it – is no easy thing. However compelling your story, there's the anxiety of whether you *can* tell it. 'I'm worried my mother [father, spouse, children, neighbours, colleagues, second cousins removed] will be upset,' students say. And no matter how often I advise them to Just Do It (and to save their worries about the ethics of publishing until they've finished writing whatever it is), they continue to fret about the rights and wrongs of telling their story. It's as if they don't feel entitled.

There are candid memoirs I can direct them to, for reassurance: not just contemporaries like Tobias Wolff, Lorna Sage, Andrea Ashworth, Eva Hoffman, Joan Didion, Dave Eggers, Linda

Grant and Julia Blackburn, but Rousseau, St Augustine and Thomas de Quincey. There are also arguments I can put to reassure them. 'If your sister disagrees with your version of events, let her write her own book.' 'You're telling the truth – what's wrong with that?' 'Not everyone objects to being written about. Some people even feel flattered.' But in the end the best bet is to ask the student: 'Have you never come across a text that spoke with such truth that you wanted to shake the author's hand? That made you feel "Oh, so I'm not the only person in the world who has thought or felt that"?' To which the answer is: 'Yes, of course I have.' And to which I then say: 'That's the kind of book you're trying to write. So go ahead. One day some reader might be grateful for it.'

Why poetry matters

In *Once in a House on Fire* Andrea Ashworth describes how reading poetry became a solace and refuge: 'My mind flitted and soared over sonnets and odes that made miserable things seem sublime.' She progressed to writing her own poetry – 'A poem was a box for your soul . . . the place where you could save bits of your self, and shake out your darkest feelings.' This is why many people start writing poems: to get things out that can't otherwise be said. The results are usually terrible: if you're writing a poem, it's not enough to shake out your darkest feelings; you have to work at them, shape them, give them form. Still, there's nothing intrinsically wrong in using writing as therapy. The therapeutic element in writing doesn't come from pouring things out or 'washing your dirty linen in public', but in finding the right words, ordering the experience, and making the story available to others. Once a poem succeeds in this way, then there's catharsis for the reader, too. When we see thoughts and feelings which we have had set down by someone else, with more clarity or candour than we would be capable of, we don't feel robbed or plagiarised, we feel relieved. Larkin's poem 'Aubade', for example, speaks of a terror of death which many people share but would feel too awkward to own up to. It gives voice to the bleakest of feelings, but does so with such elegance that its bleakness becomes consolatory and affirming.

It takes courage to own up to dark thoughts and dangerous feelings. But poetry – the most intimate yet public of forms – is the ideal place. Ted Hughes is one writer who recognised this.

Writing, he said, was about facing up to what
we were too scared to face – about saying what
we would prefer not to say, but desperately need
to share. Poetry, he said, was:

> nothing more than a facility for expressing
> that complicated process in which we locate,
> and attempt to heal, affliction – whether our
> own or that of others whose feeling we can
> share. The inmost spirit of poetry, in other
> words, is at bottom, in every recorded case,
> the voice of pain – and the physical body, so
> to speak, of poetry, is the treatment by
> which the poet tries to reconcile that pain
> with the world.

In Hughes' case, the great challenge was
learning to speak of his marriage to Sylvia Plath,
and how it went wrong, and why she committed
suicide – matters on which journalists and scholars
felt free to pass opinion, but which he kept silent
about until, at the end of his life, he published the
Birthday Letters. Not all the poems in that collection are models of candour and directness, or
indeed of artistry. But the best of them are terrific.
And, for Hughes, writing them was a huge relief.
'I had the sensation of the whole load of long

preoccupation dropping away,' he told Seamus Heaney. All the painful memories he'd been hiding, 'from myself and everybody else', no longer seemed terrible at all.

The poems in the *Birthday Letters* are intensely personal. 'Remember how we picked the daffodils?' one poem begins. 'Nobody else remembers, but I remember.' The memory is his alone. But by recording it as he does, in moving detail, he lets the rest of us in on it, and deepens our understanding of love, hope, grief and loss.

Another reason why poetry matters

Poetry is associated with profundity – with the uttering of thoughts that lie too deep for tears. Perhaps that's why some readers feel scared by poetry: they worry they'll be out of their depth. But not all poets set out to be deep. Some work skittishly, for a laugh. And others offer the pleasure of formal accomplishment, rewarding us with complex metres and cunning rhymes. Poetry is a serious business, but it isn't solemn or funereal. All it insists on is that we read carefully, with concentration. The shortening of lines is a signal to slacken our pace:

Caution all prose hogs!
The poem is a speed bump.
It's there to make you slow down.

Reading catatonically

Two years ago, buying a birthday present for my wife in a jeweller's near Chancery Lane, I was mugged. The police thought the muggers had taken me for a diamond merchant, which I found surprising, even insulting. Whatever the case, they must have been disappointed when they opened my backpack: all it contained was a shirt, a pair of socks, a washbag, copies of three of my books (I'd given a reading the night before) and Francis Spufford's *The Child That Books Built*, which I'd only just started. There was no replacing the marked copies of my books, which was annoying, but I reordered Francis Spufford's online – consolation and restitution of a kind.

Browsing through it the other day, I found the passage I'd been reading before I was mugged:

> when I read obsessively as a child I was
> striking a kind of deal that allowed me to
> turn away. Sometime in childhood I made a
> bargain that limited, so I thought, the

power over me that real experience had . . .
Twenty-five years have gone by since then.
My life has changed, and so has the content
of my reading. But the bargain holds. Still,
when I reach for a book, I am reaching for
an equilibrium. I am reading to banish pity
and brittle bones. I am reading to evade
guilt, and avoid consequences, and to limit
time's hold on me . . .

Francis Spufford's wasn't an unhappy childhood, but his little sister had a life-threatening
illness and his mother developed osteoporosis at
thirty-two. Losing himself in a book – 'reading
catatonically' as he puts it – became his way of
coping with these travails. To read so as to limit
the power that the real world has over us: is there
a better reason?

Company and solitude

Eva Hoffman's *Lost in Translation* recounts the
difficulties she has in adjusting to life in North
America after moving there from Poland. She
feels an outsider, a misfit, a stranger in a strange
land. But when she starts reading American
fiction, her sense of isolation disappears:

People are often lonely in American novels, and can't easily talk to each other; they flub human contacts horribly, and tend to find themselves in seedy rooms, alone, or out on the frontier, grimly questing. As for men and women, they either speak to each other with great sentimentality, as in *For Whom the Bell Tolls*, or find each other truly disgusting, as in *Miss Lonelyhearts*.

Being an alien myself in the midst of all this alienation turns out to be no disadvantage.

You might want to quibble with Hoffman's definition of the American novel. But she touches on something profound here: how literature creates a sense of companionship. In solitude under the reading lamp, we meet characters who are themselves solitary types. And as a result, we feel less lonely.

For myself, I like quiet when I'm reading, with no one else around. 'Go Away: I'm Reading' is the slogan on a mug I'm fond of, and on my office door, at Goldsmiths College, is an image of Johannes Gutenberg, brow furrowed, hunched over a book – my hope is that any student who sees it will imagine I'm similarly occupied behind the door and won't knock unless their errand is vitally important. But there are also times when I leave the door open, or when I wish my mug carried a second slogan on its reverse side: 'Join Me: Let's Read Together.'

When you're deep into a book, it's for yourself alone. But once you've finished, if it's any good, you want to share it with others – rehearse the story, assess the characters, discuss what makes the book special. Children do this instinctively, and the growth of book clubs, reading groups and blogs reflects a continuing and perhaps increasing need for adults to share books in this way.

There's no contradiction. First engage, in private; then exchange, in public. Both ways of interacting with a book are valid and pleasurable. As is being read to or reading aloud.

Forbidden pleasure

Some of us grow up in homes where reading is notionally approved of, because 'educational', but in reality gently discouraged. My father made me feel guilty if I had a book in my hands, because it meant I'd no hand free to play tennis with him or help wash his car; the problem with reading, as he saw it, was that it didn't involve physical exercise or the performance of useful practical tasks. Lorna Sage's mother was similarly oppositional, dusting the books of her vicar-father but never opening them, since she associated them with his errant ways. Lorna did open them, and felt her grandpa coming back to life 'whenever I communed with the dandyish and despairing characters in his leftover library'. She also opened the books owned by her Uncle Bill, 'enchanted by their news of forbidden love, civil wars, corsetry through the ages, incest and necrophilia'.

'Forbidden' is the key word. Just as some of the most powerful books ever written have been *samizdat* (works banned by the government of the day, and produced in conditions of secrecy or exile), so the experience of reading is often most intense when it's surreptitious – when we feel we shouldn't be doing it, either because the book in question is in some way illicit or because reading itself, for whatever reason, has been outlawed. Andrea Ashworth recalls naughtily reading *Tess of the d'Urbervilles* by the light of her pencil torch while working as a cinema usherette ('I read on, obsessed by the idea that I was tainted, like Tess'). And for Seamus Deane, in his novel-cum-memoir *Reading in the Dark*, books are likewise a shadowy pursuit. Ordered to stop reading at night, he would 'switch off the light, get back in bed, and lie there, the book still open, re-imagining all I had read, the various ways the plot might unravel, the novel opening into endless possibilities in the dark'.

The canon

If reading is most charged when the pleasure we take in it is illicit, where does that leave the canon? Don't people get turned off books when they're set texts? Aren't lists of improving literature self-defeating? Isn't the best way to encourage reading counter-intuitive, by proscribing books rather than prescribing them?

Well, up to a point. In an engaging new book, *The Pleasures of Reading in an Age of Distraction*, Alan Jacobs has some gentle fun at the expense of American literature professors who publish self-improvement manuals with titles such as *How to Read a Book, The New Lifetime Reading Plan* and *How to Read Literature Like a Professor*. Jacobs compares their methods to those of Charles Atlas, with his body-building programmes. 'For heaven's sake, don't turn reading into the intellectual equivalent of eating organic greens,' he pleads, and urges people to read at whim, not be intimidated by experts.

Still, in the end Jacobs admits that a whimsical or random approach to reading won't quite do. Some books are simply better than others. Or last the course longer. Or grow richer the more they are reread. If we see the canon not as a social-conditioning or moral fitness programme, imposed from above, but as a collective of writers' and readers' enthusiasms, then there's no reason to resist. We might prefer to go off-piste. But there are times when a list of recommendations can be useful. And since the canon is, or ought to be, ever-changing, we can contribute to its formation by suggesting books that deserve to be better known.

The more, the merrier

Sometimes places prompt the same sensation that books do: we feel at home there, as if they were created specially for us. If these are places off the beaten track, we're usually keen for them to remain well-kept secrets, fearing they'll be ruined if too many other people discover them. Books aren't like that. We've no investment in keeping them to ourselves. Let the whole world have them. The world will be the better for it. And the words will remain the same.

Carmen Callil

―――

True Daemons

Like most people born in a wealthy country, in practical matters I had a most fortunate childhood. My vast family live in Melbourne, Australia, and our branch of it very near the beach coast on the bay that opens out to glance at Tasmania, then goes on to face the Antarctic. We had hot, hot summers – very long ones – and short, arctic winters. This is the kind of weather that most encourages reading: it is weather to disappear from, with a book. A great deal of my reading was done in front of our Kosi wood-burning stove or the open fire, or sitting in the sea to keep cool, with a book in my hands.

My father was a barrister. He was a lecturer in French at Melbourne University, spoke Arabic and was familiar with a number of other languages. He was also a gambler – dogs, horses, cards, backgammon. In a sense he was a book gambler too, because as an avid collector, he often bought books in auctions. Amidst the pile of books, sold in lots, there would be the one he wanted. But all the books came home to us.

My father died of Hodgkin's disease, lymphoma, when he was forty-eight and I was nine. It takes some time to die of Hodgkin's disease; he was ill for some years and so I hardly remember him, and before he died I was sent to the convent. Each of his four children reacted to his death in different ways. In my case I retired to the vast collection of books he had left behind. Most of them were on shelves all around our sitting room, on either side of the fire one needed so much in the winter. The surplus was to be found in piles in a shed in the garden, where my mother also put up a ping-pong table for my brothers and me to humiliate each other in endless competition. There were more in the outhouse next to the laundry, together with gigantic piles of the *Saturday Evening Post*, which taught me about Tugboat Annie, Norman Rockwell and baseball – all, except for the paintings of Rockwell, so inferior to the Australian traditions my ancestors gifted me. *Reader's Digest* was another source of information. From that I learned about Spoonerisms, the marvellous disarray of words that constituted the speech of the

Reverend William Archibald Spooner: 'Mardon me padam, but you are occupewing my pie' and 'Spring is here and chirds are birping.' The latter became a family phrase to describe any good day.

Travelling from left to right, in the mind's eye of my nine-year-old self, I can see again the books on the library shelves. On the left of the window that looked onto the verandah were the French books. So different from English books, marked by the simple covers, the red or black lettering, the absolutely assured appearance of the publications of Gallimard or Flammarion, Plon or Grasset. These were on the left of his desk, at which I sit now to write about his books. To the right of that was a mysterious section, remembered now for two items: an *Encyclopaedia of the Body and its Works* kept high on a top shelf, out of reach of us children, and discovered only at that time when a young body does *not* want to see diagrams of instruction as to where to place the penis or position the vagina (but would prefer to learn by practice).

Also there was C. M. Doughty's *Travels in Arabia Deserta*, a beautiful edition, which I opened constantly and failed to comprehend for many years. But as the volumes were so beautiful – heavy, covers encrusted – this did not matter to me. Doughty was surrounded by books about strange places and tomes in Arabic, which one could make neither head nor tail of.

Then came the fireplace, and to the right of that, stretching around to the doors opening onto the hall, was my favourite section. These shelves were full of novels, books of philosophy and nonsense, biographies, plays and poetry. Prominent were Shaw, Meredith, Wells, Dickens, Chesterton, Belloc, Baring. There were hundreds more, and considerable miscellanea which fascinated me, in particular the works of George Borrow, a formidably eccentric Bible-basher, traveller and recorder of the Gypsies and hoi polloi of nineteenth-century England. Despite the dreamlike nature of his adventures, Borrow is always forthright. He was my close comfort after the death of my father. My copies of *Lavengro, The Romany Rye* and *The Bible in Spain* are annotated first by my father, and then by me:

> When a man dies, he is cast into the earth,
> and his wife and child sorrow over him. If
> he has neither wife nor child, then his
> father and mother, I suppose; and if he
> is quite alone in the world, why, then,
> he is cast into the earth, and there is an
> end of the matter.

(*Lavengro*)

There were strange editions of the *Prophecies* of Nostradamus, naughty paintings of bosomy ladies by Norman Lindsay, and a book that set my mind in solid plaster: *Some Lies and Errors of History* by the Reverend Reuben Parsons, DD (1893). This is a collection of essays written from a Catholic point of view, essays of the ilk of 'The Truth about the Inquisition', attacking 'the misstatements of all modern enemies of the Church concerning this tribunal . . . Whenever humanity carries out a great design, it becomes prodigal of blood', and 'The Last word on the Massacre of St Bartholomew's Day' ('the number of the victims has been greatly exaggerated'). Another delight was *The Oyster: Where, How and When to Find, Breed, Cook and Eat it* (1861). ('There is something poetical and pretty in the idea, which once prevailed, that the oyster was a lover of music . . .' and 'Arrived in port, the oyster first truly becomes sensible of the miseries of slavery . . .')

Books of peculiarity and wonder sat on these shelves. It was these odd books with which I spent most of my time, and they extended to the shelves to the right of the doors to the room. And there were collected many of the bits and pieces acquired in the auction job-lots. Key among them, for me, was the autobiography of F. C. Burnand, *Records and Reminiscences, Personal and General* (1904). Who on earth was he? In finding out, I introduced myself to Gilbert and Sullivan (not difficult to do anyway, because their operas and songs generally were much loved in the Australia of my childhood). F. C. Burnand was a comic fixture at *Punch* and editor of it from the 1880s, and wrote the libretto of *Cox and Box* for Arthur Sullivan. *Punch* cartoons, Gilbert and Sullivan, the novels of George Meredith and the travel writings of George Borrow hardly prepared me for the reading environment I was to enter next: the convent.

It was the sort of Catholic convent that should have been in deepest Ireland, but was in fact in one of the more elegant Melbourne suburbs. I was sent there when I was eight, and from it I was disgorged at sixteen. The Loreto nuns who educated me were semi-enclosed, which meant no speech from dusk to dawn, Mass every morning at 6.20 a.m., a tomato for supper on Sunday nights and much Irish brown bread the rest of the time. Rules, censorship and silence, and above all a sense of disapproval waiting to pounce on those rare times when you felt most entirely yourself. And an obsession with sin. What sort of sin? Answers came there none.

In the convent it was more a matter of what we could not read, rather than what we could. Our reading matter has been chronicled so many times by so many other fellow sufferers it hardly bears repeating. My worst memory is the stories of the Catholic martyrs read out to us at breakfast. The most ghastly story, which calcified my heart, was that of Roman soldiers putting to death a particular saint who was whipped to death by the *uncus*, a rope to which were attached sharp iron hooks. The hooks buried themselves in her skin and the soldiers then pulled away her flesh. Such things turned me into a morbid child.

However, I was saved by my mother. Left a young widow with the four of us, she managed as best she could. She had to be a stay-at-home, or wanted to be, so reading was a most important part of her life. She had the library of course, but she strayed further than that in her reading. We had all the basic literature of every Australian child: the poems and novels of bush and city, stories of bushrangers, explorers, bunyips and kookaburras, drought and the sea. To these were added Biggles and William, a most perfect combination of childhood reading. In the winter months she read out to us as we sat around the stove. These were the years of Dickens: *Great Expectations, David Copperfield, The Pickwick Papers.*

My mother had an excellent and thoroughly English sense of humour. She was very attached to the witty parson Sydney Smith and to Hesketh Pearson's biography of him *The Smith of Smiths* (1934). Among Smith's many aperçus was 'Live always in the best company when you read.' This my mother and I did: we read for company, but decided for ourselves what was good or not. To this day I do not move outside the house without a book; inside my house they are my paintings, my decorations, my fellow travellers and my comfort.

Another maternal favourite was the father of the Sitwells, Sir George Reresby Sitwell (1860–1943), an aristocrat who abused his children and everyone else who came within his bailiwick. She was particularly fascinated by his reactionary opinions and methods of topiary. My mother died when she was ninety-one, and she read till her eyes gave out. We corresponded about books; I have thousands and thousands of letters from her, and also, surrounding me – in addition to my father's desk – many of his books, which she packed up and sent over to me when she finally came to accept that I had settled in London. Her eye for the out-of-the-way and her sharp sayings have stood me in good stead too.

I had arrived in London by 1960 and five years later, with good and bad luck, I had begun to work in book publishing. I was a 'publicity girl', then one of the few jobs available to women who did not want to be secretaries. It was the Sixties, those most reviled years, but to me nothing but a decade of nonchalance, friendships and discovery. Work was my drug of choice and, in those days, it felt as though anybody could do anything. Life in London in the 1960s, a most excellent time to be young, added to my childhood fodder. We were libertarians, and the feminism that raised its head in those years was part of it.

How often I remember sitting at dinner tables in the 1960s, the men talking to each other about serious matters, the women sitting quietly like decorated lumps of sugar. I remember one such occasion when I raised my fist, banged the table and shouted: 'I have views on Bangladesh too!' George Borrow would have done exactly that. One day, when having a drink in a pub in Goodge Street, the idea for my publishing company came to me like the switching on of a light bulb.

I would publish books that needed to be

published, books forgotten or neglected, books I would ferret out and make available, perfectly certain that there were thousands like me who would buy and read them. So in 1972 I founded Virago, to break a silence, to make women's voices heard, to tell my mother's stories, women's stories: my stories and theirs. Women's history, not only histories of men at war; books that celebrated women and women's lives. Modest ambitions. I always believed that books change lives, that writers change lives. I also believed – still do – that injustice corrupts those who indulge in it, and I wanted change for our brothers, husbands, uncles, fathers too.

The first Virago books were published in 1975: history, memoirs, a wide range of non-fiction. Then in 1977 the writer Michael Holroyd insisted I read Antonia White's *Frost in May*. This novel, about a nine-year-old girl closeted in an English convent, is funny, beautifully written, its heroine a young Everywoman up against an authoritarian and frightening body of adults who insist on subduing her spirit in the name of God. Rosamond Lehmann used to tell me how often the readers of her novels wrote to her exclaiming, 'This is my story.' *Frost in May* was mine. I had to republish it.

How could I publish *Frost in May*? The answer came quite easily: here were the celebration and fun I was looking for, here was a way of illuminating women's history in a way that would reach out to a much wider audience of both women and men. I would publish a multitude of novels, I would publish them in a series, I would market them as a brand, just like Penguin. If one novel could tell the story of my life, there were scores more, and thousands of readers who would feel as I did. *Frost in May* became the first Virago Modern Classic, a library of treasures now more than 500 novels strong.

My inspiration was always literary. It was books and writers and writing I loved. Childhood beliefs and instructions from those in power above disappear as children grow to adulthood, but the comfort of books and reading is stalwart. Only particular books or writers can disappoint, but the gift of information and entertainment is always there, night and day.

The writer who perfectly conveys this is Philip Pullman in his trilogy, *His Dark Materials*. His heroine is a young girl, Lyra Belacqua, who lives in a world both like our own, yet entirely different. As adventure stories, fantasies, the three novels are masterpieces of storytelling. But they encompass radical ideas, the most remarkable of which is Pullman's concept of daemons. Daemons could perhaps be seen as a modern interpretation of guardian angels, but in Pullman's novels they take the form of animal companions, who represent the very soul, the true personality of each human being. If separated, both human and animal daemon die.

Books are the true daemons: not the imaginary animals of Pullman's brilliant imagination, but solid blocks of paper and print pottering along with you every moment of the day. There for you. Books are shields against a terror of boredom, that curse of most childhoods. What they offer does not change, and if the human race was separated from words and thoughts and stories, it would die. I took that legacy from my childhood, but more: a habit of comfort and enquiry. If something happened to me, if I felt something, I would go to books to read about others' experiences, others' thoughts, to find out what to do and what to think. Books tell you jokes, make you laugh, laugh with you.

Every age has always encompassed great change. In the fifteenth century – when Gutenberg's invention of moving type enabled words on the page to become printed books, cheaper to produce and available to the world at large rather than to the learned or monastic few – my guess is that the reaction to this transformation was much the same as the dire warnings we hear today about the possible disappearance of the book.

It is illogical to think that my experience with reading and books is unique. It is what writers write, the words on the page, that are important. But reading a book is only one way of communicating with a writer and the thoughts he or she has put down in words to entertain, educate or amuse us. The technological marvels that allow us to download books or print a single copy at the press of a button are additions to, not subtractions from, the pleasure of reading. Books don't disappear; they remain on shelves, solid, earthed objects in a modern world that has now entered the stratosphere of the Internet, broadband, iPads and e-books.

It may be that books in the form of a printed publication will shiver for a decade or two, but they will never disappear. There they are, in libraries and homes and schools all over the world. Reading a book on a Kindle or an iPad is all very well – in fact it is better than all very well, it is splendidly practical – but it is not the same. A machine can never *look* like a book: books are far more beautiful. Books are like gardens; a Kindle or an iPad like a supermarket – it makes life easier, but one doesn't want to loiter in it. You can fiddle with books. Like gardens, they can be wonderful to look at. You can cuddle them and use them like a hot-water bottle; a machine can't do any of these things.

It is often said that the modern world provides no time to read. But this is not the case. Until the twentieth century the majority of the human race expended every ounce of energy and every moment of the day struggling to get enough to eat. Vast tranches of the world's population still live like this today, but for most of us born into fortunate lands we have so much more time to play, to lounge about, to entertain ourselves. This is very recent, yet the human race has been telling stories and trying to record them on papyrus, on manuscripts, on stones, since the beginning of time. Whether we read on the printed page or on a machine is beside the point. It is the ideas and stories that count. Books, light-bulb ideas about publishing them, children who use them to make sense of life will always exist. The human race will read for as long as it survives on this Earth. And books and reading stand there like the largest defensive army in the history of world, showing us how to do that. Publishers of books, be it in print or on the Internet, are the foot soldiers of this army. On they go, on they must go.

Tim Parks

Mindful Reading

Maybe we can start by reminding ourselves what a strange art form writing is.

For there is no artefact as such: unlike painting or sculpture, there is no image to contemplate, there is no object you can walk around and admire. No one is going to say you must not touch. No alarm will go off if you get too close.

You don't have to travel to enjoy a piece of writing.

And there is no performance, either. Strictly speaking. Unlike concerts or plays, you don't have to queue for tickets or worry whether you're near the front.

You can't take a photo.

Then a book has no fixed duration. Unlike music, you don't have to respect its timing, accepting, along with others, an experience of the same length.

You can't dance to it. You can't sing along.

Instead, there are signs on paper. Or on a screen.

We can change the size, or shape, or colour of the signs, we can alter their distribution on paper, on the screen. We can divide them in pages or, if we want, on the computer we can unite them in one unending page, or one unending line.

Because the signs are not the art itself.

We can read in Baskerville or Bookman, in Arial or Calibri. Bold or italic. Capitals or not. Doesn't matter.

We can read these signs at whatever speed suits us, stopping and starting again wherever we want, for however long we want; we can leave our book for a tea break, a shopping trip, or a week's skiing, and still come back without having changed anything.

Only the *sequence* of signs matters. The *writing* is in the *sequence* of the signs. This is the one thing we can't change. The experience is the sequence. The experience is not in any one moment of perception, but in the movement through the sequence from beginning to end, at our own speed, with interruptions. At the beginning of each sentence we are projected towards the end. At the end we have the momentum of the beginning. Same with the paragraph, same with the chapter, same with the whole book, maybe the trilogy. The beginning requires the end, the end the beginning. We are locked into a journey.

Let's admit the dangers.

When we arrived in this world, before we rightly knew what was going on, they were already filling our heads with words. We came to something we call *consciousness* hearing words. We started to copy words. We realised that making certain sounds in certain sequences would get us what we wanted. Certain formulas expressed pleasure, others displeasure. Soon the words seemed as natural as our cries and shouts and breathing and eating.

They weren't.

We could barely walk before they put books in our hands. Now they wanted us to imagine the sounds *silently*, constructing them from visual signs, subtracting them from the give and take of company. Alone. Adults read alone, withdrawn, the mind full of words that have no material existence.

Soon the sounds became *pure mental phenomena*. Unheard. Unspoken. If we wish, we can memorise whole sequences of signs, from a book, we can learn them off by heart. If you choose, you can have a poem entirely in your head, without ever having heard it aloud. In your head, the remembered poem is *exactly* the poem on the page, not like remembered music or remembered painting, or sculpture, or film, which is necessarily different from the thing itself.

You can say that remembered poem to yourself as often as you choose. You can recite, silently in your head, 'To be or not to be'. 'Kubla Khan'. *The Waste Land.* Or something you've made up yourself that's never been written down. No copyright law can defend poetry from memory's reproduction.

By the time we reach adolescence it is already hard to imagine active, purposeful consciousness without words. It seems a human being can't really have a full existence without this invention, this great facilitator: the word.

Reading and writing, we find we are moving in a separate system. Not the material world of the senses. The habit is compulsive. The mind's constant reception and generation of words crowds out its perception of physical phenomena. Absorbed in words, we loosen our grip on things as they are. Or rather, we introduce a new thing into that universe: the words exist, after all, in our minds.

This mental, word-driven life is congenial. Reading silently, the words speed up. We follow the sequence faster than we could ever speak it. The eye streaks ahead. The page turns while our sense of what came before is still falling into place. Other perceptions – a distant lawnmower, a smell of fresh baking, a fall of temperature – are dulled. The world has been left behind. Instead a whirling word machine has lifted off from the heavy surfaces of soil, cement and skin. Mind and body part company.

This is the big danger: that our reading will become part of the mental feverishness, the obsessive purposefulness that drains our lives of physical immediacy, threatens our health, risks turning us into frantic compulsives.

It starts at school. Huge amounts of information need to be accumulated, through reading. We must absorb people's histories, their ideas, their metaphysics, through reading. We must cram. We must buy a pile of books and read them, when the teacher wants, when the curriculum stipulates. We must read *Hamlet* before we're ready for *Hamlet*. And Chaucer and Donne. We are given the impression that quantity is paramount. Better to have read the complete works of Shakespeare than just a couple of plays you liked. Better to have read Brontë and Austen and Thackeray and Dickens rather than just Brontë, or just Dickens. But when? These books are so long. Life is short. And there is Facebook. There is Twitter.

We start to skip. Teacher has led us to believe that we are reading *Middlemarch* for information. For an exam. The same way we are reading *Principles of New Mathematics* for an exam. Or *European History 1815–1914*. Skipping is fine so long as we come away with the appropriate titbits; so long as we find a few significant phrases we can knowledgeably quote. Our multiple-choice exam asks: 'Was *Lyrical Ballads* first published in: a) 1788, b) 1798, c) 1808, d) 1818?' Damn! Who reads the copyright page? 'Was Flimnap a character in: a) *The Dunciad,* b) *Gulliver's Travels,* c) *Peter Grimes,* d) *The Castle of Otranto?*

Hmmm.

Our reading becomes frenetic, fragmented. We confuse geography books with travel literature, novels with history, and newspapers. All that matters is our ability to gut the material and regurgitate it. After a couple of years of this we discover that when it comes to literature you can save even more time reading CliffsNotes. Why didn't we think of that before?

When we read for pleasure, if we still do, it's hard to shake the school reading habit, this dreadful acquisitiveness, this grim business of conquest and processing. Now we read for plot. We need to know what happens. And we're more impatient than ever. TV soaps are so fast. We've downloaded the whole of *Friends*, the whole of *Scrubs*. Soaps can tell a great story and get a lot of laughs in just twenty minutes. Why does it take these boring old writers so long? Trying to read Philip Pullman we receive an average of three text messages a page. We stop to reply. It's going to take for ever to finish this. But we have to read Pullman because everyone does. We need to boast that we have read Pullman. We read the books our peer group reads. Tolkien of course. Skip the songs, though. Skip the guff about Middle Earth. Skip to see if Gandalf is really dead. He can't have killed Gandalf!

And *Harry Potter*. Everyone reads *Harry Potter*. Can't remember the name of the author. Who cares? It's Harry that counts. What will happen to Harry when he grows up? Harry is our generation. Harry is us. What will happen to me? That's what I need to know. Oh, but this *Deathly Hallows* is deathly dull compared to *Scrubs*! Actually, I've no idea who wrote that either, though for some unfathomable reason that's more acceptable.

And after the *Potter* cycle, what do I read next, if I can be bothered to read anything at all? What are my friends reading? *Twilight*. What is in fashion? Vampires. What book will tell me what I have to know? The next part of the story, my story, our story.

Stop!

Breathe, relax.

Let's have a rethink about the experience books can offer. Let's try to figure out why we're not really enjoying ourselves.

A premise.

If everything we see in the world around us has its word, its name, we can also invent words for things we can't see. Make up a sound and imagine something it refers to: angel, soul, spirit, ghost, god. They exist, in words. In our heads. In our heads, with words, we can conjure anything.

One of the words we invented was 'self'.

With the words we know, silently, in our heads, we create something, an entity, a fantasy, and we call it 'self', a creature with a past and a future, in much the same way that sentences and stories have a beginning and an end. To reassure ourselves that it is really there we invented another word: identity. And another: character. And another: personality. The more words, the more our invention exists.

Self is a linguistic creation. It's hard to have a self without words.

Every self has a story. It exists in relation to other selves and other stories. In a continuum. It seeks to distinguish itself by comparing itself with others, using terms of comparison that again are all words – fear courage, good bad, happy sad, winner loser.

The self exists in a web of words spun out of the mind, separate from the world of sense.

So, these writers telling their stories, scribbling their novels, are exploiting this state of affairs. Using thousands upon thousands of soundless signs, they mimic the way we are forever constructing our lives and the lives of others, in words. They reinforce a process we are all involved in. This is why we get interested. Whether we're aware of it or not, we refer every story that we read to ourselves, our lives, because the medium of written narrative is intimately involved with the way we make up ourselves. Some stories will be liberating: Ah, such and such a thing is possible after all, despite what our friends and parents say.

Some stories will remind us of dangers: Do this and you'll end badly, mate. But wait a minute; maybe that thing I want to do is only possible in the world the writer is talking about. Not in my world. Maybe that ending badly had to do with other times, other places, not my time, not my place. Nobody's stoned for adultery in London. We have to get a sense of where a story is coming from. Context is everything. We have to remember that some of the most brilliant writers were not necessarily wise, not trustworthy.

If we read fast, superficially, for plot, to get through, so as to congratulate ourselves we've read a big book that everybody else is reading, or just to get a shot of intense feeling, we're not only missing out on certain pleasures, we're actually putting ourselves at risk, leaving ourselves open to messages and attitudes we haven't weighed up, allowing ourselves to be troubled or enthused, or even terrified, without really knowing if there's any cause to be.

What pleasures?

I'm going to say that it's learning how to take intense pleasure in reading that makes it also useful for us, really useful and really exciting. And safe, or fairly safe. So I'd better describe this pleasure well.

Enchantment is part of it. But only part. 'Enchantment', from the Latin, *incantare*, an entering into song, into chant. The opening sentences of a novel are an invitation to enter a separate world of rhythm and sound, mental activity and social positioning. They have a voice, a feeling, a direction:

> It is a truth universally acknowledged, that
> a single man in possession of a good
> fortune must be in want of a wife.

> If you really want to hear about it, the first
> thing you'll probably want to know is
> where I was born, and what my lousy
> childhood was like, and how my parents
> were occupied and all before they had me,
> and all that David Copperfield kind of crap.

> The sun shone having no alternative on the
> nothing new. Murphy sat out of it as if he
> were free in a mew in West Brompton.

However fast you like to read a book overall, make very sure you read the opening page or two with the utmost care, savouring every word, thinking about where this writer is coming from and what kind of spell she or he is trying to draw you into, how anxious he is to impress, whether he's treating you as dumb or smart, whether he's serious, whether he's fun. The first few pages of any Thomas Hardy novel will warn you that the reading experience you can expect is one of waiting for disaster to strike; if you're not up for it, there's still time to bail out. The first few sentences of any D. H. Lawrence story tell you that you'd better be ready for an argument – with the author, that is; he's going to try to ram some very heavy ideas down your throat, but he wants you to fight back. He's not interested in yes-men.

The pleasure here is of entering into enchantment *slowly*, consciously, with vigilance. Don't be a pushover. If you feel the writer's careless – he's trying to run before he can walk, he imagines you're a sucker for a bit of blood spilt in the first sentence, or in need of easy sentiment, or titillation – you have every right to resist. You have every right to put a book down after a couple of pages, which is why it's always wise to read a little before buying. Life is simply too short for the wrong books, or even the right books at the wrong time.

Basically, what I'm saying is that there are two

sources of pleasure that you suppose to be in competition with each other, cancelling each other out, but actually they're not. If you learn to blend them, they actually intensify each other.

The first, as we said, is enchantment, the business of succumbing to the way someone else constructs the world, in words, to the rhythm of his sentences, the sound patterns of his language, and the relationship of these rhythms and patterns to the things being said, the things happening in the book. It's a wonderful thing to let go of your own way of telling yourself the world and allow someone else to do it for you.

But the second pleasure is awareness, wakefulness: the capacity to see, feel and consciously register all that is going on around you and inside you. Actually, the inside and outside awarenesses are pretty difficult to separate, since your perception of what's going on outside you is something that you are always assembling inside your head. It's true the world is out there, and not in your head, but equally true that your idea of it, how it looks and feels, is a constant process of creation on your part, and that is very definitely in your head. So when I say awareness of a book, a writer, his sentences, his stories, I also mean awareness of how I am engaging with the writer and responding to him. Because, for me, his book only exists in relation to me and in my response to it. It is not an absolute.

What I'm talking about then is a pleasure that combines relaxation and effort, immersion and detachment, letting go and being vigilant – consciously savouring, if you like, the experience of letting go; or again, understanding what it means to be a person who lets go when reading this kind of book.

I fear this will sound mysterious. We need examples.

Let's say I love reading detective stories, or sentimental romances, or chick-lit. Some genre fix. I know what I'm after, I choose the right cover and blurb. The book begins the way these books always begin. I accept an enchantment I've accepted a thousand times before. I kill a few hours pleasantly enough. Maybe I relax. Maybe I read really fast because I'm already a bit irritated that I'm wasting so much damn time reading a book like a million others I've already read. Still, I know I'll do it again. Much the way I know I'll always go back to chocolate even when I tell myself not to. I love eating chocolate and, even while I'm loving it, I worry that I'm eating chocolate again. Etc. Etc.

This is one kind of reading experience. Nothing wrong with it, but nothing special either.

Now let's imagine we pick up a *Harry Potter* or, for a different age group, a Murakami, or a Salman Rushdie. Or even a classic: *Vanity Fair, Tess of the D'Urbevilles*. We know it's successful stuff. We know it's safe to say we like it. We allow the rhythms to take over at once. We sink immediately and totally into its spell. We have a wonderful experience. But at the end, as the spell wears off, we begin to realise that we don't actually agree with a lot of the lines the book was selling. We're not entirely happy about some of the feelings that were aroused. Or a friend points out some massive flaw in the plot. Now we begin to wonder whether we would have surrendered to the book so completely if it hadn't been so famous. We feel a little concerned that maybe we have no point of view of our own and just let ourselves get pushed around by the flavour of the day. Am I too ingenuous? The fact is that because novels engage with the way we construct our identities, it's important to feel you're not just a dupe for every new trick. Self-esteem has to be an issue in the way we engage with writing. To keep enjoying a book after we've finished reading it, we have to feel we were critically alert when we read it.

A little chastened by this experience, especially after it's been repeated dozens of times, we begin to be a bit more cautious of blurb and hype and peer pressure. We read with a new awareness, watching how the spell is being cast, thinking of it in relation to the way other books work, other spells are cast, succumbing maybe, a bit at a time, but also observing our succumbing, understanding ourselves better in our reaction to what we're reading, understanding our friends better who love or hate this book, taking pleasure in the story, yes, but perhaps even greater pleasure in the mystery of how we take this pleasure and how we stand in relation to this story and others. At this point even a book we don't love can be an immensely exciting experience.

Most of all, this approach sets us up for the most wonderful and life-changing reading experience of all: I mean when we come to a book with immense suspicion, perhaps saying to ourselves: This isn't what I was looking for at all, why am I bothering with this stuff? Who is this guy? Who does he think he's trying to kid? Only to discover that the writer has hooked us. He's seduced us. Damn! How did that happen? These rhythms we thought were ugly are beautiful, even breathtaking; this story we thought was boring is fascinating – no, it's essential!

So this novel, which was definitely not what you were looking for, now turns out to be *exactly* what you needed. It has allowed you to discover something new about yourself, because you were watching your reaction as you read it.

Still, we're all different and perhaps all I'm doing now is telling you who I am and how I read: with a pen in my hand, ready to write BRILLIANT!, ready to write BOLLOCKS!, fully aware that I may come back to the book a year hence and reverse those judgements. Because the excitement of reading is the precarious one of being alive now, intensely mentally silently alive, and reacting from moment to moment, in the most liquid and intimate sphere of the mind, to someone else's elusive construction of the precarious business of being alive now.

Mark Haddon

The Right Words in the Right Order

At home I still have the boxed set of six Puffin books given to me as a prize when I was a twelve-year-old pupil at Duston Eldean Junior School. *I am David* by Anne Holm, *The Dolphin Crossing* by Jill Paton Walsh, *The Silver Sword* by Ian Serraillier . . . And I would love to say it all started there, that my eyes were opened to the wonders of literature by a gift of children's classics, but I can't remember a single detail from any of the stories. I'm not even sure I read them, not least because I read very little fiction at that age. On the contrary, the book I remember reading most avidly around that time was Erich von Däniken's *Chariot of the Gods?*, a piece of thrillingly bonkers pseudoscience that explained how aliens visited the earth, destroyed Sodom by means of a nuclear explosion and gave our distant ancestors the technology to build Stonehenge – the very same aliens who are described in the Book of Ezekiel as coming out of the North in a whirlwind of cloud and amber flames in the likeness of men. I can still recall turning the pages, spellbound in a deckchair on Brighton beach in 1975. Crazy golf and 99s and the Ark of the Covenant.

When I was finally forced to admit that these things might not be true, my grief was softened by a growing obsession with books about man's fossil ancestors. *Australopithecus, Pithecanthropus, Homo habilis.* Who were, it now occurs to me, another kind of alien in the likeness of men who once walked upon the surface of the Earth, though in this case they really did give our distant ancestors the technology to build Stonehenge.

It also now occurs to me that whilst I read different books these days, my reasons for reading have changed very little. It's the thrill of being transported to another world. 'Once upon a time . . .', 'Beyond the thrice ninth kingdom . . .', 'London, Michaelmas term lately over . . .'. Like all travel, part of the enjoyment comes from learning about new customs, new languages, new landscapes, but an equal part comes from learning new things about myself and about the home I've left behind, which I can see so much more clearly from this distance.

The point being, as I sometimes say to people who write to me asking me for advice about Becoming A Writer, it doesn't matter where you start, or when. What matters is a passion for arranging and consuming words.

For me it began at fourteen when I was given two collections of verse to read for my English O-level, the *Selected Poems of R. S. Thomas* and the anthology *Conflict and Compassion* edited by John Skull. Peter Porter's 'Your Attention Please' from the latter is still lodged uncomfortably in my mind:

> Do not
> Take well-loved pets (including birds)
> Into your shelter – they will consume
> Fresh air. Leave the old and bed-
> Ridden, you can do nothing for them.

It was not simply the way these writers lit up the inside my head, but the fact that they did so by selecting and rearranging words you could hear at the bus stop. Thirty-four years later I keep having to remind myself how extraordinary this is. No rabbit, no hat, no camera, no canvas.

Select the right words and put them in the right order and you can run a cable into the hearts of strangers. Strangers in China, strangers not yet born.

It was when I decided to start reading proper adult novels that things started to go wrong. I borrowed Camus' *The Plague* from the school library and singularly failed either to enjoy it or to understand why so many older and more intelligent people had clearly enjoyed it. A struggle with Sartre's *The Age of Reason* only compounded the problem. The words remained inky shapes on the paper. I could read them in the literal sense, but they refused to dissolve and let me pass through. Worse, this feeling of exclusion remained with me when I returned to the books that had once transported me so effortlessly. And if this sense of exclusion was one of the things that inspired me to become a writer, to understand and replicate the magic that once held me spellbound, it was profoundly dispiriting at the time.

What I didn't yet understand was the importance of taste and timing. Books are like people. Some look deceptively attractive from a distance, some deceptively unappealing; some are easy company, some demand hard work that isn't guaranteed to pay off. Some become friends and stay friends for life. Some change in our absence – or perhaps it's we who change in theirs – and we meet up again only to find that we don't get along any more, an experience that I had when I returned to both *Gravity's Rainbow* and Armistead Maupin's *Tales of the City*. Unlike people, one can at least dump them or hand them to a friend without causing offence or feeling guilt. Indeed, we forget sometimes that a vital part of loving literature is hating certain books and certain writers, just as hating Spurs is an important part of supporting Arsenal; and the embarrassing truth is that I have probably got far more satisfaction out of trying to persuade friends that *The Girl with the Dragon Tattoo* is a tawdry piece of misogynistic torture porn than I have out of discussing the reasons why *Wolf Hall* is a masterpiece.

For me, specifically, the pleasure is rarely about plot, which is probably why I can't remember what happens even in some of my favourite novels. Ten or so years ago, I finally got around to reading Proust in the Penguin Terence Kilmartin translation. Halfway through the third volume I started to notice marginal scribbles in my own unmistakable hand. I had read it before and forgotten everything.

For me, the pleasure is often about finding writers and books who push boundaries, not just the outright experimental zaniness of, say, *Tristram Shandy*, or B. S. Johnson's *The Unfortunates*, which came in a box of separately bound chapters to be shuffled before reading, but books that make the house of fiction seem suddenly larger and brighter. It could be Paul Auster's *City of Glass*, in which Daniel Quinn, a writer of detective fiction, receives a misdirected phone call intended for the private detective Paul Auster and decides to take on both the case and Auster's identity. It could be Nicholson Baker's *The Mezzanine*, a love-poem to the million details of one office lunch hour. Or it could be Francis Spufford's *Red Plenty*, which is sitting on my bedside table right now, and which weaves real people and real events into a series of stories bound together by the economics of Soviet central planning during the Khrushchev era and makes of this unpromising premise something deep and warm and moving.

This is sounding like a list of recommendations, which is, perhaps, ultimately all you can do when singing the pleasures of reading. 'Try this . . . Try that . . .' It's hard enough to explain your own passion, let alone why someone else might share it.

But pushing boundaries means nothing if a writer doesn't love the language itself. A novel in which the words are used merely to convey a story seems to me a waste of words. I want to hear the instrument cherished and played exquisitely. I want to read sentences and phrases that sing on the page. And my favourite novels are often obscured by a shower of underlining and highlights:

> However dark the habitation of the mole to our eyes yet the animal itself finds the apartment sufficiently lightsome.
>
> (Oliver Goldsmith, *The Vicar of Wakefield*)

> I was a Prisoner lock'd up with the Eternal Bars and Bolts of the Ocean.
>
> (Daniel Defoe, *Robinson Crusoe*)

Consequently – and sadly – I find it hard to fall utterly in love with novels in translation, which was, perhaps, one of the problems with my early, doomed flirtation with the French Existentialists. I can enjoy the work of a writer like Haruki Murakami, for example, whose clean, clear style seems, to me at least, relatively independent of its original Japanese, but I can't read Chekhov or Flaubert in English without feeling that I'm missing something of vital importance, rather as if I were listening to a symphony rescored for piano. I can hear the melody, I can hear the harmony and the rhythm, but where are the violas? Where are the woodwind?

Which is one of the reasons why I belatedly taught myself Greek at thirty-six, and found myself taking my A-level in a gym full of teenage girls at Lady Eleanor Holles School in Middlesex, so that I could get some small sense of Homer and Euripides in the original; and why I resurrected my long-dormant Latin in order to translate some of Horace's *Odes*. But whilst these things gave me some of my most intense reading experiences – I don't think you ever read with as much appreciation or attention as when you are translating – they also made me acutely conscious of what I was missing elsewhere.

Pushing boundaries. A love of language. I also want novels to be humane and generous. Indeed, I think all good novels *have* to be humane and generous. I want to read novels which not only understand and care deeply about their flawed and wayward characters, but which also, miraculously, seem to understand *me*, whether they are *The Wind in the Willows* or *Middlemarch*.

More specifically still, I am always in search of novels that understand and articulate precisely what it feels like to be a human being. Not so much getting characters *right*, which is the entry requirement, surely, but capturing the texture of life itself. I don't think any writer has ever done this better than Virginia Woolf, and I think the way in which she does it clearly illustrates something essential that can be done in the novel and in no other medium.

She is peculiarly good at describing what happens second by second in the mind, so that the reader says, repeatedly, *Yes, yes, that is precisely what it is like to think and feel*, that roller-coaster swoop from plans for supper to the fear of dying, between childhood memories and the scent of the flowers in the hallway:

> How incongruous it seemed to be
> telephoning to a woman like that. The
> Graces assembling seemed to have joined
> hands in meadows of Asphodel to have
> composed that face. Yes, he would catch the
> 10.30 at Euston.
>
> (*To the Lighthouse*)

She is equally good at capturing those moments when the membrane between us and the world stretches almost to transparency and everything seems suddenly bright and clear and true:

> And the audience turning saw the flaming
> windows, each daubed with a golden
> sun; and murmured: 'Home, gentlemen;
> sweet . . .' yet delayed a moment, seeing
> perhaps through the golden glory perhaps
> a crack in the boiler; perhaps a hole in the
> carpet; and hearing, perhaps, the daily
> drop of the daily bill.

(Between the Acts)

More deeply still, she understands how the human self is not something constant and contained, but how we exist sometimes within our bodies and sometimes outside, how we can be utterly divorced from everything, then unexpectedly find ourselves melting into objects and rooms and landscapes, how a part of ourselves is always contained in other people:

Yet there are moments when the walls of
the mind grow thin; when nothing is
unabsorbed, and I could fancy that we
might blow so vast a bubble that the sun
might set and rise in it and we might take
the blue of midday and the black of
midnight and be cast off and escape from
here and now.

(*The Waves*)

No other medium can articulate this, the
experience all of us have of being a single human
mind with all our prejudices and blind spots and
distortions, yet this being the only point of view
from which we can observe the universe.

Lay the novel alongside film and its special-
ness becomes obvious. Film promises everything.
Ancient Rome, dinosaurs, talking dogs, car
chases, sex, Mars, vampires . . . Such a boundless
cornucopia that we forget what it can't do. It
can't do smell or taste or texture. It can't tell
us what it is like to inhabit a human body. Its
eyes are always open. It fails to understand the
importance of the things we don't notice. It can't
show those long stretches of time when we are

seeing nothing at all, just drifting in our own minds. Film can't show how you and I look at the same face and see two different people.

Stop reading right now. Look around you. It doesn't matter if you're lying in bed or sitting in a crowded Tube carriage. This is what film can't do. The sense of being *inside* looking *out*, of seeing a world that belongs to everyone, but is nevertheless yours alone. It is this uncrossable gulf between me and not-me, between my private experience and yours, which lies at the heart of being human and which no other medium can touch, and this border is where the novel lives and moves and has its being.

Which is why the novel will endure, much as it has endured in the face of film, television, censorship, political persecution, second-hand bookshops, online selling, the demise of the small bookshop and the rise of Amazon . . . not just because it offers refuge, companionship, excitement and edification, for there are other ways in which we can get these things, but because it does a unique and extraordinary thing that nothing else can do, a unique and extraordinary thing that lies very close to the mystery of what it means to be human.

It's tempting to say more. It's tempting to

move seamlessly from recommending to pros-
elytising, to turn the cheerleading into a mission
with a moral dimension. Writers, teachers, librar-
ians, publishers . . . books changed our lives.
And because the passion we feel about reading
is so strong, and because we are good people,
we sometimes fall into the trap of believing that
books made us into good people and that they
can do the same thing for others. This, I think,
does a disservice both to readers and to the
books themselves. Partly because of the snobbery implicit in the phrase 'good books' –
meaning, of course, the ones that you and I
enjoy reading. Partly because there are so many
things that can change lives: boxing, learning
to play the piano, tending an allotment . . . And
partly because it's not true. Visit a prison library
and you'll meet good people whose lives have
been saved by potboilers, and psychopaths
reading Jane Austen.

I would love to say that reading possessed
some of the special powers it is often claimed
to possess, not least the ability to soothe the
troubled mind. But when my mind is troubled,
like many people, I find reading hard, if not
impossible, and fiction in particular becomes a
country from which I feel painfully exiled, so

that when I'm able to read again it feels like coming home.

Talking about reading as the *cause* of anything is to get things back to front. It exists in the valley of its own making. It gives us pleasure; and our embarrassment about pleasure, our fear that reading is fundamentally no different from sex or sport, tempts us into claiming that reading improves us. But pleasure is a very broad church indeed, and we do literature no great service if we try to sell it as a kind of moral callisthenics.

Reading is primarily a *symptom*. Of a healthy imagination, of our interest in this and other worlds, of our ability to be still and quiet, of our ability to dream during daylight. And if we want more people to enjoy better books, whatever that means, we should concentrate on the things that prevent people reading. Poverty, poor literacy, library closures, feelings of cultural exclusion. Alleviate any of these problems and reading will blossom.

For these, I think, are the real threats to reading; not technology, not the pervasive and rising fear that readers are being tempted elsewhere by the shallow pleasures of *Britain's Got Talent* and *Call of Duty: Black Ops*.

Indeed, we forget that the novel in English is a relatively new art form (*Robinson Crusoe*, 1719, *Pamela*, 1741; travel writing, science fiction and the picture book are all older), and that for a large part of its life it has attracted the same criticism now directed against TV, films, computer games and the grubbier reaches of the Internet. Novels dragged readers into private worlds that were hard to monitor and police. They aroused violent emotions, reduced social interaction, blurred the line between fantasy and reality, and required insufficient mental effort, thereby softening the impressionable minds of those who did not have the requisite moral strength: women, children, the lower orders. As *Punch* wrote of the nineteenth-century sensation novel, 'It devotes itself to harrowing the mind, making the flesh creep, causing the hair to stand on end, giving shocks to the nervous system, destroying conventional moralities and generally unfitting the public for the prosaic avocations of life.'

I have no idea what's going to happen to publishing over the next forty years, and anyone who claims they do is a fool. Forty years ago I was using my father's slide-rule and thinking that the automatic sliding doors on the *Starship Enterprise* were thrillingly modern. The Internet would have seemed not just vanishingly unlikely, but beyond comprehension. God alone knows what 2050 will bring.

Given the speed of technological change, it's fitting that while writing this essay I've been looking at Faber's iPad app of *The Waste Land*, which includes a filmed performance of the poem by Fiona Shaw, synchronised readings by Eliot, Ted Hughes, Alec Guinness and Viggo Mortensen, original manuscript pages, academic interviews . . . It is the most wonderful thing. And given the speed of technological change, by the time the essay is published you'll be able to download something even more extraordinary. Books can piggyback on these huge technological changes in a way that other art forms can't, because they're digital, and have been from way before Gutenberg, a string of symbols that can be transmitted in any medium. Turn *Half a Yellow Sun* into Morse code, then spoken English, then British sign language, then binary, bounce it off a satellite, turn it back into written English again and you haven't lost a thing.

The way in which we make and consume images has been changed utterly by Photoshop and its relations. Pro Tools and the like have done the same for music. Turn on the radio, open a magazine and you're hearing sounds and seeing pictures of a kind that simply could not have been made in 1980. It is rare now to hear a film score played by a real orchestra or to see a hand-drawn animation. I recently watched *The Social Network* and didn't realise that the Winklevoss twins were played by one actor, despite appearing together in most of their scenes. But if you read *Clarissa* on screen, you're reading what Richardson wrote, give or take some academic quibbles over spelling and textual variants, because a novel is just the right words in the right order.

And that, for me, is the most magical part of the trick that holds us spellbound. Films, paintings, sculptures . . . these things are finished products, more or less. But a novel really is just inky shapes on paper. It comes to life only when we read it. And we all read differently. You may think you know Maggie Tulliver or Esther Summerson, better than some members of your own family, and I may feel the same, but you and I know very different versions of those characters. Because reading is never simply reading. Reading always involves writing too. A novel is an invitation to complete an imaginary world. If the novel is good we do it without batting an eyelid.

Films and television programmes, plays and paintings and sculptures never really become friends in the way that novels do. We can admire, we can be impressed, we can be moved and consoled, but we rarely feel that peculiarly personal attachment we feel to a loved novel, because whilst writing novels is a long and solitary business, reading them is always a collaboration, and a good writer gives the reader space and encouragement to play their part so that when we close the final page we have had an experience that is partly of our own making. We create our own Maggie Tullivers. We create our own Esther Summersons.

A few weeks ago I read Padgett Powell's *The Interrogative Mood*. It has no plot, which is, of course, fine by me. It is composed entirely of questions, and is therefore outrageously experimental, though without the coldness and contrivance that undermines many experimental novels. It is gorgeously written and chock-full of so many underlinable delights that I might as well just quote the opening paragraph:

> Are your emotions pure? Are your nerves
> adjustable? How do you stand in relation
> to the potato? Should it still be
> Constantinople? Does a nameless horse

make you more or less nervous than a
named horse? If before you now, would you
eat animal crackers? Could you lie down
and take a rest on the sidewalk?

It is humane, peculiarly attentive to the work-
ings of the mind and oddly satisfying as
a whole, though why this should be so, when
most of the questions seem utterly unconnected,
was initially a mystery. Was there some hidden
structure? Does the reader gradually and
unknowingly piece together a jigsaw of the
writer's secret life?

And then it dawned on me. You can't help
reading a string of questions that are addressed
to you without answering them, which is
precisely what I found myself doing. Some of
the questions had no answers and some had
obvious answers with no resonance. But some
made me dredge up memories that had been
buried for a long time, and a few made me probe
parts of my mind where I'd never probed before.
And I began to realise that this strangest of
books was the best example of something as
common as rain, something shared by every
good book I have ever read. This wasn't a
monologue. This was a conversation. The secret

biography was my own. It was a book about me. And if you read it, then it will be a book about you.

In an interview after the novel was published Powell was asked who the narrator of the book was. He answered, memorably, 'Dude, c'est moi.' He was wrong, I think. The correct answer was, 'Dude, c'est toi.'

Michael Rosen

Memories and Expectations

We are on holiday on the coast of Yorkshire not far from Whitby. It's a campsite and there are two families with a couple of friends added in. This is 1959 and I'm thirteen. Just as it's getting dark we are called to the biggest tent where my father is pumping up the tilley lamp, a large green light that works by burning paraffin under pressure in a 'mantle' – a white cylinder of cloth that sits at the top of a tube. He loves faffing about doing this, and that's what he calls it when he pretends it's bothersome. 'It's a bit of a faff,' he says whilst adoring the way that it's his expertise with the paraffin can, the funnel and the little brass handle that delivers this hard, white light.

So we sit ourselves down on sleeping bags, blankets and cushions. The tilley lamp sits on a fold-up wooden chair, my father sits on another in the middle of us. Looking round the tent, I can only see our faces catching the light, as if we are just masks hanging there, our bodies left outside in the dark perhaps. In my father's hands is a book – *Great Expectations* – and every night, there in the tent, he reads it to us. Without any hesitation, backtracking or explanation he reads Pip's story in the voice of the secondary-school teacher he is, but each and every character is given a flavour – some more than others: Magwitch, of course, allows him to do his native cockney. Thinking about it now, I can see that his Jaggers was probably based on a suburban head teacher from one of the schools he taught in; Uncle Pumblechook could have been derived from the strangely pompous shopkeepers and publicans who peopled the hardware stores and cafés of outer London, where we lived in the 1950s. But over the years, as my father tells us about his own upbringing, some of Dickens' characters start to mix and merge with our own relatives.

There is someone called Uncle Lesley Sunshine who, like Pumblechook, turned up in my father's home when he was a boy to offer advice and hold out prospects of betterment. This was London's East End, a terraced house in one of the streets behind the London Hospital in Whitechapel, where my father and his sister were being brought up by their mother, Rose, along with her mother and father, and it's where several (how many? more than we could ever count) of her sisters and brothers live, too. Lesley Sunshine seems to have dropped into this crowded world from some other well-heeled sphere in order to take the 'boy' to places where he will be improved, like a tailor's, who, because he is a relative, will fit the boy out in a decent bar-mitzvah suit for free.

Rose has plans of her own for the boy. Somehow, in ways that my father never found out, she summons people from another world into their home. On occasions seamen from Russia, Jamaica and America would find their way to their kitchen. At the time my father didn't know how or why they got there, but looking back, he could see that they were people she had met at meetings and they would sit in the tiny space of that home talking to her own father, who had arrived from Poland, and to my father, who was of course a boy. It was mysterious and different from his friends' homes and gave him a contradiction to figure out: how come he appeared to be living in such a poor, tiny place, but people from all over the world would choose to come there? It gave him a mix of shame and pride to deal with. His mother would also take the boy to the local Whitechapel Library, which had become a kind of international centre for the uplifting of the masses, and this too was a place that opened a window on the world and a door to a future life away from the area. The air was full of people speaking different languages, whispers and rumour passed around, that this or that great back-street scholar was writing a masterpiece over there; the great painter and poet Isaac Rosenberg had sat just here; this or that revolutionary or preacher or teacher was just over there behind the shelves. Some of that was true, but a more powerful if more mundane truth was also at work: it was here that poor boys and girls from migrant cultures were finding their route through the literature and science that would take them to the sixth forms and universities they yearned for. My father's journey began with a little book about whales, which he took home and pored over, and ended with Milton. More mysteriously, on one occasion, Rose and the boy got on a tram and travelled north to Belsize Park, a place so different, so luxurious as to appear to him as somewhere foreign. There she took him to a flat, where one room was as big as a whole floor in their house. On the walls were paintings of a woman with no clothes on, her skin yellow, her face still. There were books everywhere and, between the books, pots and carved figures. In the middle of it all sat someone grand, a woman wearing strange clothes who spoke in a voice that came from another place or from another time. This, he was told, was someone important; perhaps there was a prospect that she could help the boy, and he had to be on his best behaviour. So he sat on a chair while Rose and the woman talked about Communism. It turned out that this woman and the yellow woman with no clothes on were one and the same person – Beatrice Hastings – and the painter was Modigliani.

Thinking back to the tent and the tilley lamp, I can see Pip walking up the stairs, following Estella, to see Miss Havisham on what would be his life-changing climb, a moment that would alter his whole perspective on who he was, what he wanted to be and how he would view others. Beatrice Hastings was no Miss Havisham, but there is something swirling around in both my father's mind and mine, mixing and blending when I think of the lone woman in a room with these haunted ties to a man from the past. In fact, I can't really sort out who's who, real or imaginary, and I think this is how we all read when we have time and space to think about books.

What I mean is that of course Dickens told us about a Miss Havisham whom he created, but when many of us read about that Miss Havisham, we bring her to life with the Miss Havishams we know in our own lives. I think, in my case, this imaginative leap was given an extra kick, first from the way my father read the book, giving the voices and the scenes such a potency from the place and the way he read it to us, but also because both he and my mother filled our minds and lives with such vivid stories and experiences. The slow, measured reading of the book, the talk and replays of the scenes and the accounts of these people end up as a kind of portrait gallery of pictures that have the ability to change places, so that when I think of Beatrice Hastings – whom I never met – at times she is replaced by Miss Havisham, and when I think of Miss Havisham I can imagine that Modigliani painted her.

My father, back in the tent, packs a lot of power into the moment when Miss Havisham tells Estella to 'beggar' the boy when they play 'Beggar My Neighbour'. He seems to especially love Jaggers; the way Jaggers toys with Pip, clearly knowing more than he lets on about Pip's mysterious benefactor. He relishes the descriptions of Wemmick's peculiar house in Walworth

– coincidentally, where my father taught at one of the new inner-city comprehensives. These characters have a life beyond the tent. They are quoted and referred to as we go about the camp-site. If I'm sent off to buy some eggs in the village, my father puts on a Jaggers voice and says, 'How much do you want? Forty pounds? Thruppence?' When we get up in the morning, my parents are scurrying around looking for the bread or pulling the milk out from under the eaves of the tent, saying, 'Vittles, gimme vittles, boy!' It doesn't have to be an accurate quote. My father's perform-ance had given such life to the characters that their vocabulary became ours, and they could now live with us on the campsite and, it turned out, beyond, for years after. Quite out of the blue, my father or mother would transform themselves into Pumblechook, calling out: 'And three! And nine!' as if I was Pip and they were calling after me through the railings of Miss Havisham's house.

The character that my father brought most vividly to life was Trabb's boy, a young chap who works for the local tailor and who is the first to spot Pip's efforts to distinguish himself from his lowly background, mocking him for his apparent snobbery. To be honest, at the time I didn't under-stand the significance of Trabb's boy. I couldn't really see the humour in this little chap walking down the street with a pretend cape over his shoulders, calling out, 'Don't know yer!' For my father, this seemed both incredibly funny and especially poignant in ways that I couldn't see or reach. Why, when he was quiet, prodding the fire, or if we were walking on the moors, would he suddenly say, 'Don't know yer!'?

Years later he gave a hint as to why this might have been. He said that there was a boy at school called Rosenberg – David Rosenberg, I think. He showed him to us on his class photo. Rosenberg was, he said, his best friend. But the Rosenbergs were poor. Quite how you could be even poorer than my father, his sister and his mother, I could never understand. After all, Rose had on occasions taken my father to various charities in order to ask for school boots. Both my mother and father talked of the tenements and flats that surrounded them while growing up as being full of bedbugs and grime. My mother hated dirt and could spot it a mile off, whether it was under a table, along the top of a cupboard door or on my face. So I thought, listening to my father, that maybe the Rosenbergs had bedbugs and dirt. Even on their faces. Rosenberg, it seems, had been my father's friend, but then at some point someone else became his best friend, Moishe Kaufman. Indeed, not only did Moishe Kaufman become his best friend, but Moishe Kaufman's girlfriend, Rene Roder, became the best friend of my father's girlfriend, Connie Isakofsky. They were a foursome and David Rosenberg wasn't part of it. In the shuffling of the pack of these East End boys, each in their different ways got what they needed to leave this place, to move northwards or eastwards to get out of this poverty and foreignness, to become less 'heimish,' as it was called – the 'heim' being the mythical far-away place in Eastern Europe where everyone looked and talked like their grandparents, lived in tiny houses and kept chickens. At some point David Rosenberg got frozen out. But something went deeper than that. There was some moment, some event, some incident, which I never fully heard about or understood, where it seems as if, to my father's great regret and shame, he did something or said something to David Rosenberg – perhaps he pretended not to know Rosenberg, cold-shouldered him, looked down on him. It was a Trabb's boy moment and I can now see that my father must have recognised himself in Pip, trying to leave his past behind and better himself.

So, wrapped up in that gesture that my father

did when he played out Trabb's Boy was a mockery of himself. Trabb's boy was doing what I presume David Rosenberg didn't do, which was act out the snobbery that he saw in my father. To do it on a campsite in Yorkshire in 1959, some twenty-five years after that scene or event that had taken place in a dingy, inky 'Foundation School' on the Mile End Road, may, I suppose, have helped him banish the guilt – well, at least for a few seconds.

In the end, my father did a Pip on nearly all of his family. We used to visit Rose – a tired figure he called 'Ma'. We saw his sister Sylvia, but that was about it. In their place was a set of names, the kinds of names you never heard in the London suburbs of the 1950s – Raina, Lally and Busha – only as real as characters in a novel. We were in John Lewis; this wasn't somewhere we went very often. In fact, I think it was the first time I had ever been there, though I understood that there were places my parents thought of as rather special: quality places where you could buy tasteful things. John Lewis was one of the places you could go to get such things, and Heal's was another, and as a result chairs and carpets and curtains appeared in our flat in the suburbs with patterns and designs and colours that I never saw in other people's houses. Perhaps there was a touch of the Beatrice Hastings about the things they tried to acquire. The long arm of my father's own Miss Havisham determining how he thought about curtains. Anyway, in this place, John Lewis, a woman stopped my father and said, 'Is it Harold?' They talked for a few moments. She seemed tall and posh and imposing and then off she went. Who was that? That was his Aunty Rene – her real name was Raina. My father looked bothered and distracted by it.

So, perhaps in Trabb's boy's 'Don't know yer' were Raina, Lally and Busha. I never knew exactly why we weren't part of them, or they not part of us. There was a suggestion that some of them were locked in an old religion, full of what he thought were pointless beliefs. But there were times when he would show regret that he hadn't kept on with Chanukkah, Purim and Seder nights, and he would talk longingly of dishes we had never tasted, strudel and *charoseth* and *humentaschen*, and fun things like giving away bits of bread before Pesach or hunting matzos.

So as *Great Expectations* got read and re-enacted, and these re-enactions were absorbed and reabsorbed into our family life down through the years, I could see various characters and situations in the book intertwine with these missing people. Alf, whom we didn't ever see, was lovely. My father loved Uncle Alf. He talked of his kindness and the special treats. He was a lovely man, he would say. So was he a Joe Gargery figure to my father? Or, in his mind, was his loving grandfather the Joe figure who kept the stern aunts at bay, those aunts who seemed always in my mind to be frowning at the boy and complaining that he was getting the tastiest bits of the chicken – the 'fliegel' or the 'pulke'. These women were all at once Pip's sister, bringing him up 'by hand'.

Of course there doesn't have to be a like-for-like match between people. Part of the power of stories is the way in which we can see facets of this or that fictional person in the people we know, and scenes from the fictional world have echoes in the events of the real world. As the book, and my father's reading of the book, and my feelings about the book developed, I felt from him a sense of yearning. Pip is desperate to get away from his old home and, once he's had a sniff of what Miss Havisham appears to offer, he follows the dream of a better life. My father had some kind of dream. It was that his father would turn up and take him away from these horrible aunts. His father would arrive from America in his swell car, in his swell suits, and say, 'Hey, Harold, let's make tracks.' And he would drive down Nelson Street in a convertible while all the family and the kids with their bedbugs and dirty faces would watch open-mouthed. But his father never came. Morris Rosen stayed in America. Rose never said bad words about him. He had special things to do. He was a union organiser. He was standing for the State Senate of Pennsylvania for the Socialists. He was organising support for Sacco and Vanzetti, who had been framed and would be executed. He was busy. So he never came. But the yearning stayed until my father was old enough to realise that he never would. By then, like Pip, he had become what one of the relatives had called a 'psy-college boy'. He had studied English literature – books like *Great Expectations*. When I too came to do the same thing, I saw how so many things had ended up getting intertwined here: my father's performance of the book; how the scenes became part of our daily lives and language; how all this spoke to me about the kind of family my father had come from and the changes he had been through before I was in this world. Books can do this. I'd also say that there is an added dimension, when books leave the page and become spoken out loud in a room full of people: of course they become live and vivid, but they also become social, they end up belonging to everyone in the room (or tent) at that moment. My father also read us *Little Dorrit*, Walter Scott's *Guy Mannering* and, much later, most of *Catcher in the Rye* and *Catch-22*. Even more memorably, he also read out loud his own memoir, which he called *Are You Still Circumcised?*

A few years ago I went to Boston because I had found out where Morris Rosen was buried. It was on a long road through the north of the city. I walked past tattoo parlours and empty car dealerships until there were no more buildings, just waste depots and cemeteries. It was November, cold and raining, and I found the graveyard, the 'Jewish Workmen's Circle Cemetery'. And there was Morris Rosen. On his grave it said 'Beloved father'. 'Beloved father? Beloved?!' As one of my relatives replied, 'Haven't you heard of Jewish humour?' There was also a number on the grave: the number of the branch of the Workmen's Circle, the self-help organisation that Jewish workers set up. It was number 666. For several days I scanned pages on the Internet trying to find where branch 666 was. In the end I found it: Mattapan. Boston's biggest mental institution.

So there in the graveyard was where all that misplaced yearning had ended up, with a number representing the name of an 'asylum' on it. No Magwitch came out from behind any gravestones while I was standing there, but in a way all my cemeteries are Magwitch cemeteries. That's how my father in the tent in Yorkshire goes on working.

Jane Davis

─────

The Reading Revolution

Literature and Time Travel, I had called it, in
hope of getting some younger, some different
people.

I was thirty-two, with my recent PhD tucked
into my belt, relatively new to teaching, and my
students in the Extra-Mural Department at the
University of Liverpool seemed to me very old.
Most of them were surely over fifty, but on the
plus side they were interested in the literature,
and I came to see them as brave voyagers. Time-
travelling, we visited the farms and pastures of
thirteenth-century England with *Piers Plowman*,
walked with Wordsworth and demobbed vagrant
soldiers in rural Cumberland, and in Charlotte
Brontë's *Villette*, with our poor French, battled
against loneliness and paranoia in a foreign
nineteenth-century town. In other words, I could

have been done under the Trade Descriptions Act, for despite the title, this was a course of reading in canonical English Literature.

The real USP, though I didn't advertise it, was that I knew *nothing*, almost literally nothing at all, about most of the texts that were to occupy our attention. This was literature for beginners with an ignoramus sitting at the lecturer's desk. The only things I was confident about were my ability to read the text (and not even that, in the case of *Piers Plowman*), to engage people in conversation and to bring an applied personality to whatever was up for discussion.

I taught in this way in that Extra-Mural Department for fifteen years. During that time, working alongside a couple of like-minded colleagues, I built up a large, loyal following of people who were willing to read in this inexpert, exploratory way. Often, what was being read was as new to me as it was to my students. Usually we read large portions of the text aloud in the class, to make it lively and present in our minds while we talked about it. That concentration on actually reading the book – here, now, in the room, together – was to become the cornerstone of *Get Into Reading*, the shared-reading model I developed when I founded The Reader Organisation in 2002.

Devoted individual readers, solitary and private, look away now. I'm going to suggest changing – or at least adding a new model to – the way you read.

The Reader Organisation's *Get Into Reading* programme develops read-aloud groups that meet once a week, with children as young as three and with people over ninety, taking place in youth clubs, high-security psychiatric settings, work-places, dementia care homes, drug rehabs, schools, day-centres, libraries, corporate boardrooms, prisons, supermarket cafés. It's a reading group, but not as you perhaps know it.

In shared reading the text, poem, novel, short story, play or whatever is read aloud, in its entirety, by one or more members of the group. The group talks about the book as it is read, freely interrupting the flow of the reading with personal responses ranging from 'My granddad had a dog like that' to 'I didn't know anyone could explain how it feels to go into battle as he's doing here – it was like this when I . . .' (both responses to *War and Peace*). Read in this way, a short poem might take half an hour, a short story two hours, *War and Peace* eighteen months.

The model has profound implications in the realms of the personal and social, in terms of education and health: much of The Reader Organisation's work has been paid for from NHS and social-inclusion budgets. It would be a mistake, though, to see shared reading as something only for sick or unhappy or economically deprived people. It has simply been easier for us to develop projects in those areas where the need is most obvious. But *the need*, in our fractured society, is everywhere. It is time that shared reading reached the mainstream.

As you are reading this book, it naturally follows that you are an accomplished and dedicated reader. You think of reading as an individual, even a solitary activity, one that you would want to defend as such, because usually, for devoted readers, the act of reading is deeply private. I'm going to argue, though, that even highly proficient readers might want to try shared reading, which is in equal measure about books *and* people. It isn't just about getting non-readers into reading (though it does do that remarkably well); it is about building relationships out of communal meanings. Sharing a book is a multiplier, as anyone who has ever read, night after night, to a story-besotted child will know. It is about mutual recognitions, the sharing of selves. Let me give an example.

We had a good first term in that time-travel class, and celebrated with a Christmas party to which all the travellers brought food and favourite poems to read aloud. Pat, a university administrator, an imposing lady who reminded me of a jolly headmistress – capable, but good fun, and utterly *together* – read 'I Am' by John Clare. Written in a lunatic asylum, where Clare was incarcerated, the poem is very moving:

> I am – yet what I am, none cares or knows;
>   My friends forsake me like a memory lost:
> I am the self-consumer of my woes –
>   They rise and vanish in oblivion's host
> Like shadows in love-frenzied stifled throes
>   And yet I am, and live – like vapours tossed
>
> Into the nothingness of scorn and noise,
>   Into the living sea of waking dreams,
> Where there is neither sense of life or joys,
>   But the vast shipwreck of my life's esteems;
> Even the dearest that I loved the best
>   Are strange – nay, rather, stranger than
>   the rest.

I long for scenes where man has never trod
   A place where woman never smiled or wept
There to abide with my Creator, God,
   And sleep as I in childhood sweetly slept,
Untroubling, and untroubled where I lie
   The grass below – above, the vaulted sky.

When she had finished reading there was an appreciative silence, followed by people making some remarks about the poem, but then Pat said (I paraphrase from a probably faulty memory), 'This poem means a lot to me because I used to live on a farm in Australia and I became an alcoholic. I became so much of an alcoholic that I lost my marriage and my children . . . lost everything.'

She described, in brief and with a cool, resolute lack of self-pity, her life as an alcoholic who had lost everything. And then went on, 'And during that time, which lasted some years, I had this poem. I kept it all that time on a scrap of paper in my pocket, and I used to take it out sometimes and read it, and think, yes: I am. I am.'

This was time-travel indeed, this strange shared process that took feelings and thoughts in and out of individuals, in and out of time and place, and connected it and us all up: John Clare, Pat, the other students, me; Northampton General

Lunatic Asylum, the streets of Melbourne, this Liverpool University seminar room, 1845, 1975, 1990. The room was charged with a powerful energy, the poem electrifying as we listened to Pat read it. It was the most moving thing that had happened to me in my career as a reader and a teacher of literature and it happened at a Christmas party, not in class: we were there as people and fellow readers, off-curriculum.

Look at the life-saving equipment John Clare packed into this poem of human wreckage: 'I am' it begins, a great stone slab of assertion. How powerful those opening words are when I imagine being in a state – 'the vast shipwreck of my life's esteems' – where who and what I am seems utterly insecure. Giving voice to the unbearably true, and *knowing it* in full consciousness, is like having proof of reality: 'yet what I am none cares or knows', most helpful, however painful, when you feel unreal, ungrounded. Clare is not afraid of going deep into his trouble in the second stanza or of imagining an alternative reality – an impossible, damaged, but beautiful vision of a fresh start or even the relief of death – in the beautiful and saddened third.

I wonder now, how had John Clare's poem worked for Pat all that time she was in thrall to her addiction? Did reading it do her good in the pain of it? How could a poem help your life? Keeping hold of stuff when you are down and out is hard, people tell me: you are always on the move, you have to carry what you've got, and you often have to leave places sharpish. But she had the poem (first read in an anthology she'd won as a prize at school), and she'd kept or refound it and held onto it because it was valuable. The poem's very existence, on its scrap of paper in your pocket, tells of other worlds, worlds you might once have inhabited, worlds you may one day wish to find or refind. Read the poem alone and you have your own experience and imagination to touch the poem into life. Read it with six others and you have six lives and six imaginations with which to inhabit this flexible human-shaped space. You also have something non-literary: the growing connections between and among those six people.

Though I knew something powerful was happening at that Christmas party, I 'had the experience but missed the meaning', as T. S. Eliot puts it, for the significance of the moment didn't become clear to me until many years later, when I began to recognise it as part of a phenomenon that occurs when people are reading aloud and together, in a particular way. It is to do with the three-sided connection between the text, the personality (which may be more or less explicit) of the person who is reading, and the people sharing the listening, in a kind of personal amplification. The reverberation of Pat's story has remained part of the poem for me, always there in the background, and I find the poem the more powerful because of the recollection and imagining of Pat's alcoholic (and recovered-alcoholic) setting. That anyone might have lived those three very different lives (farmer's wife, rolling-stone alcoholic and university administrator) and that they might all be held together by John Clare's verses changed the poem for me, for ever.

I think of this story when anxious people challenge me about reading 'serious' literature in our shared-reading groups. Why not, they will often say, read *lighter* stuff – surely easier for people who aren't feeling too happy, or who have different social norms?

The plea for lightness may be a natural and entirely understandable fear of getting serious: lots of us spend a great deal of time not thinking, for fear of being brought down. Often, too, the person who imagines the 'lighter stuff' as being more appropriate – and in my experience this has included the GP, the prison governor, the librarian, the HR manager, even the literacy tutor – that person, often in authority, is still simply afraid of the word 'literature' and especially afraid of 'poetry'. I'm not sure that anyone *in* the world of literature knows how far *out* of the world of literature most people are. It's perfectly likely that, if they didn't do English at A-level (and most people don't), a senior NHS manager, a child-protection officer, a forensic psychiatrist, a clinical psychologist or police chief will never have read a classic novel or any poetry whatsoever. It says something about the way we see literature that no one finds this either surprising or alarming. At the other end of the literature-experience spectrum is the professional scholar, for whom reading is impersonal and abstract, and almost always deliberately cut off from life as we live it. It is easy to see why, when dealing with literature or life stuff, people think it better if we stick to the surface of things and splash around up there, lightly pretending there are no depths, when the depths seem either unplumbed and terrifying or, on the other hand, intimidatingly aesthetic, to do with a specialist, professionalised and narrow form of education.

In this cleft stick, buying stuff is one way of

getting by, but Wordsworth put even that impulse into poetry in 1806:

> The world is too much with us; late and soon,
> Getting and spending, we lay waste our
>   powers:
> Little we see in Nature that is ours;
> We have given our hearts away, a sordid boon!

That natural desire for pleasure is why addictions can get such a strong hold on us: getting all sorts of stuff, from alcohol to new trainers, can make you feel momentarily happier. But try as we will, we cannot ignore or shout down what Wordsworth calls 'our hearts', and consistently ignoring the inner life has put depression and anxiety high among the world's most serious epidemics. Depressive disorders are the fourth-highest cause of disability worldwide. In people aged eighteen to forty-four depression is the leading cause of disability and premature death.[1]

Wordsworth argues in the *Preface to the Lyrical Ballads* that human creatures live primarily in and by feelings – and that's why we need poetry. Thoughts, he says, are what happen when feelings settle down in us through repetition: as coal is to forest, so thought is to feeling. Positive psychology is opening up new areas of thinking in these fields, and I am impressed by the thinking of Professors Layard and Seligman, of the happiness and well-being movements[2]. But readers of poetry already know that such ideas have often been the subject of explicit *literary* thinking, in the sort of deeper language, the language seeking depth, to be found in Matthew Arnold's 'The Buried Life' (1852):

> Fate, which foresaw
> How frivolous a baby man would be –
> By what distractions he would be
>   possess'd . . .
> Bade through the deep recesses of our breast
> The unregarded river of our life
> Pursue with indiscernible flow its way . . .
> But often, in the world's most crowded
>   streets,
> But often, in the din of strife,
> There rises an unspeakable desire
> After the knowledge of our buried life . . .

Despite our (perhaps also natural) desire to amass, consume and be mindless, the 'unspeakable desire' to know 'our buried life' is ancient and implacable. If we ignore it, or have no means of knowing it, that desire will come back and hurt us, as do all unmet primal needs. For Matthew Arnold, as for many people, the way to the buried life is through connection with another human being, an experience that animates powerful feeling:

> Only – but this is rare –
> When a beloved hand is laid in ours,
> When, jaded with the rush and glare
> Of the interminable hours,
> Our eyes can in another's eyes read clear,
> When our world-deafen'd ear
> Is by the tones of a loved voice caress'd –
> A bolt is shot back somewhere in our
>   breast,
> And a lost pulse of feeling stirs again.

But this is rare indeed. And ours is what sociologists call 'a low-affect society', interested in excitement, but wary of expressed feeling. Literature offers an alternative place to recover such lost feelings; and a shared-reading group offers the community in which to do that together. Since Pat's reading of John Clare's poem, over the past twenty-five years, I have often seen or felt the bolt 'shot back in the breast' when part of a group of people is reading together.

Another example: I went to pitch the idea of a Reader in Residence to a group of managers at an NHS specialist mental-health Trust. A man sitting at the table was introduced to me as John, a service-user rather than a manager.

John said to me, 'I've brought a poem with me and I'd like you to read it at some point.' I uncharitably assumed that John had brought me a poem of his own, and I agreed in a half-hearted way, and hoped we would run out of time before the moment came up. (You'll think this is cruel, perhaps, but I have been the editor of a literary magazine for ten years and have read more execrably bad poetry than most people have read newspapers.) The meeting proceeded, a meeting in an NHS meeting room: institutional furnishings, institutional carpet, even some institutional art on the wall. I spoke about what the Reader in Residence would do: the value of reading, the depth of poetry. It is hard to convey in the abstract what we really do at The Reader Organisation, but I have to try to do so. Some of the managers asked practical questions, outcomes, logistics, budgets. The meeting wore on.

'Would you read the poem now?' said John, and pushed a piece of paper towards me. It was a Gerard Manley Hopkins poem, one of the so-called 'terrible sonnets'. John told us he had been an English teacher, but that life in a failing comprehensive school had brought on a nervous breakdown. He said, 'I'll never get over it. I'll never be able to . . . go back to it.' This was a man of perhaps fifty. His sense of being unutterably broken looked very real. He told us that the poem helped him hold himself together when things were very bad. He showed us that he had a copy of the poem taped to the back of his diary. He said, 'Sometimes, if things are very hard, I can take it out and read it.' And he added, 'I can see that Hopkins managed to get it down, what I feel, in the lines. He got it all in an order: it's not the chaos. And that helps. Could you read it out?'

I read:

> No worst, there is none. Pitched past pitch
> of grief,
> More pangs will, schooled at forepangs,
> wilder wring.
> Comforter, where, where is your comforting?
> Mary, mother of us, where is your relief?
> My cries heave, herds-long; huddle in a
> main, a chief
> Woe, world-sorrow; on an age-old anvil
> wince and sing –

Then lull, then leave off. Fury had shrieked
'No ling-
ering! Let me be fell: force I must be brief'.

O the mind, mind has mountains; cliffs of
fall
Frightful, sheer, no-man-fathomed. Hold
them cheap
May who ne'er hung there. Nor does long
our small
Durance deal with that steep or deep. Here!
creep,
Wretch, under a comfort serves in a
whirlwind: all
Life death does end and each day dies with
sleep.

I read the poem with seven pairs of eyes on
me, and felt my voice crack as if I would cry at
the lines 'O the mind, mind has mountains; cliffs
of fall / Frightful, sheer, no-man-fathomed'. Such
powerful, revealing language to be using at a
meeting table in this NHS building; such true,
painful thoughts to be putting to senior mental-
health practitioners and managers: 'Hold them
cheap may who ne'er hung there'. And to be
reading it to John, whose eyes were locked onto

my face as I read, the eyes of a man awaiting, what . . . ? The public exposure of some customarily unadmitted truth. As when Pat read 'I Am', it seemed almost dangerous, as if the air again were cracking with human electricity, or John had handed me some sad powerful magic, and I'd set it off by reading it aloud, a sort of spell. Despite the institutional furniture, we are primitive creatures in a cave. We have the magic of language. It is frightening and good. When I look up again some people around the table have tears in their eyes.

I don't expect many NHS meetings go like that. But we got the contract, and still work in that innovative NHS Trust, where many clinicians, nurses, service users, occupational therapists and NHS administrators now run weekly shared-reading groups – thirty-eight reading groups every week, at the last count. Should we keep it light? John would say we should keep it truthful.

Over the last 100 or so years the loss of the religious as a reputable discourse in common life has led to a poverty of language, and thus to a poverty of contemplative thought and feeling about what we are, and what we need. We need some inner stuff, scaffolding to help us get around our inside space, something to help us map, explore and even settle those places where we are still primitive. Beliefs help in the so-called well-being indices: people who are members of faith-groups are more likely to flourish than those who are not. For the rest of us, what are we to do with that unnamed place, space, sense? What is that part of being human which is touched by silence, which recognises an intense atmosphere when people are moved, which gets scared or exhilarated when alone in a big space, or when faced with a newborn baby? Science may gradually work this out: that is our mainstream model these days for accredited seriousness, for what we can be confident in believing. But literature – too often now dismissed or misplaced – has always known that buried part, and in thousands of ways.

It is not the medics or the psychologists who refuse to see this – on the contrary, the problem is that the best literature has been for too long (affluently) ghettoised on courses and in high culture, with too little human meaning actually acknowledged. One example: a well-known broadcaster can say this, of all things, in the *Observer*:

> Being brutally honest, the only thing
> reading literary fiction qualifies you for is
> dinner-party conversation. Despite this,
> children who read early are seen as mini-
> geniuses. We're told that once we digest the
> classics we unlock the secrets of the
> universe, but there are days when I wish I'd
> learned to fix a boiler or basic electrics.
> Literature may be revered in high places,
> but most writers I've met are pretty useless
> at anything else. So we should be grateful
> there are intelligent children and adults out
> there for whom books don't appeal and
> whose skills lie elsewhere.

It may be honest, but it is brutal, even when trying to sound cute. In the face of this rather representative treason, I conclude, unashamedly, on behalf of a reading revolution.

We must reposition literature in settings – such as workplaces, mental-health services, dementia care homes, looked-after children services – where its profound worth will be seen for what it really is: the holder of human value, human meaning, and, yes, even the secrets of the universe. The growth of materialism over the past 200 years, and the development of a sense of entitlement to happiness, has created the misapprehension that if you are not happy there must be something – medically, physically – wrong with you. Many ordinary people who don't go to the GP for a diagnosis of depression are unhappy, ill at ease, at a loss, sad. This is what we used to call the human condition. But what people instinctively know, and science is beginning to understand,[3] is that what makes people happy, above all, is a network of supportive fellow creatures, a sense of purpose, challenge and meaningful occupation. Shared reading can provide all this. Get a few people together, pick up a good book and try it.

1 http:// bestpractice.bmj.com
2 *Happiness: Lessons from a New Science*, Richard Layard (Penguin); *Flourish: A Visionary New Understanding of Happiness and Well-being*, Martin Seligman (Nicholas Brealey)
3 Seligman argues that well-being is a construct with five measurable elements: positive emotion; engagement; relationships; meaning; and achievement.

Jeanette Winterson

A Bed. A Book.
A Mountain.

I am lying in bed reading Nan Shepherd's *The Living Mountain*. This is a kind of geo-poetic exploration of the Cairngorms – a mountain range in north-east Scotland. The book was written in the 1940s, and lay unpublished until the 1970s. Now it has been reissued by Canongate.

Reading it seems to me to explain why reading is so important. And odd. And necessary. And not like anything else.

There is no substitute for reading.

To go back to the book.

Nan Shepherd never married and never lived anywhere but her native Scotland in a village at the foot of the Cairngorms. She was well educated and well travelled but she always came home. She loved the Cairngorms. She wrote, 'The mind cannot carry away all it has to give, nor does it always believe possible what it has carried away.'

I am not a mountain climber or even a hill walker. I know nothing about the Cairngorms. The book was sent to me and because books and doors both need to be opened, I opened it. A book is a door; on the other side is somewhere else.

I found myself wandering the mountain range in the company of Nan Shepherd. She is dead but that doesn't make any difference. Her voice is as clear and fast-flowing as the streams she follows to their source, only to find that the source always points inwards, further. There is always further to go.

I like it that I can lie in bed and read a book about mountain climbing. There are two dominant modes of experience offered to us at present – actual (hence our appetite for reality TV, documentaries and 'true-life' drama) and virtual – the Web. Sometimes these come together as in the bizarre concept of Facebook: relationships without the relating.

Reading offers something else: an imaginative world.

I don't want to confuse this with fantasy or escapism. For me, the imaginative world is the total world, not a world shredded and packed into compartments. For the poet Wordsworth, the job of the poet and the poem is to 'see into the life of things'.

This cannot be done if we are only separating. Imagination allows us to experience ourselves and our world as something that is relational and interdependent. Everything exists in relation to everything else. The reason that *The Living Mountain* is a 'good' book is that it takes a very particular and tiny subject and finds in it, or pulls out of it, a story about how we can understand the world.

The book is a metaphor, yes, but it is also specifically about the Cairngorms. The opening it makes in the mind is its capacity to connect the specific and the local with the universal (and as Robert Macfarlane points out in his lovely introduction, the universal is not the same as the general).

A medium other than the book could not achieve the effect of this book nearly so well. A book lets you follow a writer's mind. Reading does not move in linear time in the way that a movie or even a radio piece does. Of course there is a beginning, a middle and an end, but in 'good' books that is irrelevant. We don't remember the books that have mattered to us by the chronology of their story-telling, but by the impression and effect of the story and of the language used to tell it. Memory is talismanic. We hold on to what we need and let the rest go. Just as in our own lives events separated in time sit side by side in memory, so the effect of a book is to let us live nearer to total time than linear time allows.

Linear time is exhausting. Life has never been more rushed. This present way of being is not a truth about life or a truth about time; it is propositional. We can disagree.

Part of Nan Shepherd's lifelong relationship with the mountain is to stop rushing to the top of the various plateaus of the Cairngorms. At first it is all about the exhilaration of the ascent. How far can she go? How fast? Then she starts circling like a dog with a good nose. She finds that she wants to be in the mountains. 'Often the mountain gives itself most completely when I have no destination, when I reach nowhere in particular, but have gone out merely to be with the mountain, as one visits a friend with no intention but to be with him.'

To cross the threshold of a book is to make a journey in total time. I don't think of reading as leisure time or wasted time and especially not as downtime. The total time of a book is more like uptime than downtime, in the way that salmon swim upstream to get home.

We have lost all sense of home – whether it's the natural world, our only planet, or our bodies, now sites of anxiety and dissatisfaction, or our scrabble for property in vast alienated cities where few can afford safety, peace, quiet, even a garden.

How can a book get me home? It reminds me of where home is – by which I mean I am re-mapped by the book. My internal geography shifts, my values shift. I remember myself, my world, my body, who I am.

The remapping is sometimes overwhelming – the wow factor of those books that we know have changed our territory – but usually it is much more subtle, and more of a reorienting. I feel settled in myself. To put it another way, I am a settler in myself. I inhabit my own space.

I had a rough childhood. I left home at sixteen and for the next ten years physical home was a provisional space, not permanent, rarely secure. During that time I discovered that books gave me a way of being at home in myself. They provided a shining centre – and if that sounds a bit mystical, I suppose it is, but we all have to find a way of being, a way of living, and as far as I am concerned, life has an inside as well as an outside. Most, if not all, of our time and energy goes into life on the outside – jobs, money, status, getting and spending – and this is disorientating. And it means that if life on the outside is a mess, as it often is, or unsatisfactory, we have no inner resources to help us through.

Books work from the inside out. They are a private conversation happening somewhere in the soul.

Often then, still, now, always, if I can use the book as a compass I can right my way. Reading calms me and it clears my head. In the company of a book my mind expands and I find myself less anxious and more aware.

This happens in the interaction between me and any, every encounter with a book that has being. And a book that has being is a book where the writer has found something essential and can communicate it to me.

It really doesn't matter *what.* The Cairngorms or *Wuthering Heights. Cloud Atlas* or *Moby-Dick. Zen and the Art of Motorcycle Maintenance* or a Carol Ann Duffy poem. Poetry is all about being, and because we are much less concerned with the subject matter or the story of a poem, it is easier to understand Susan's Sontag's remark, 'A work of art is not just *about* something; it *is* something.'

The is-ness of art, its being, is vital. What it is about may be interesting and absorbing, may be topical, may be urgent, but over time what comes back to us, sustains us, is none of that. Art, and that includes writing, is not an end in itself; it is a medium for the soul.

You need not believe in the gods to believe in your own soul. It is that part of you that feels not obliged to materiality. I do not know if the soul survives physical death – and I do not care – but I know that to lose your soul while you are alive is worse than death.

I want to protect my soul.

Reading isn't the only way to protect your soul, or to live in total time, or to find your own way home – but we're talking about reading here, and my most intense experience is with and through language. I am like Adam and I need to name things. This is not taxonomy and it's not reductive, rather it's trying to find a language that fits. Fits what? Not only the object or the experience but also the feeling.

It is impossible to have a thought without a feeling. Impossible not to feel. You can suppress and distort your feelings, you can displace them and be dishonest about them, but like it or don't like it, you are feeling something every second. Nothing mystical here. In the economy of the body the limbic pathway takes precedence over the neural highway. We are designed and built to feel.

When I can find a language for my feelings I can own them and not be owned by them. I can be enriched as mind and emotion work together instead of against each other. Art, all art, is good at this essential relationship, but literature finds us the words we need. And we need words. Not empty information. Not babble. Not data. We need a language capable of simple, beautiful expression yet containing complex thought that yields up our feelings instead of depriving us of them.

You only get that kind of language-possibility through reading at a high level; that doesn't mean difficult or abstruse – quite the contrary. What we think of as difficult is often only unfamiliar, so it can take a bit of time to get into a book. Reading is becoming a casualty of the surf-syndrome of the Web. Reading is not skimming for information. Reading is a deeper dive.

Or a high climb.

Nan Shepherd talks about the exhilaration of

altitude. The air is thinner. The body is lighter. But you have to acclimatise. You have to acclimatise yourself to books.

I am aware that reading is new. Mass literacy doesn't really start until the mid-nineteenth century, and we have had an uneasy relationship with reading ever since. Lots of people don't really read and don't want to read.

I think that is to do with education and cultural expectation. There is a wonderful group called The Reader Organisation, run by Jane Davis, who is a cross between Bob Geldof and Florence Nightingale, with a bit of Nanny McPhee thrown in. Her reason for living is to take reading into places where reading does not go – prisons, housing estates, children's homes, etc. She works in Liverpool with people who have often had no real schooling. Her results are incredible. Kids calm down, guys grow up, harassed mothers find themselves mirrored in Sylvia Plath and Shakespeare. There is no dumbing down offered. Against received wisdom, by which I mean received stupidity, her crazy project works. The Reader has no direct government funding.

When I left home I didn't find hope in realistic docu-drama narratives of deprived kids with no choices or chances. I found myself in Aladdin, Huck Finn, Heathcliff, the Little Prince, Henry IV. I identified with Hotspur because of course I identify with the outsider. And soon enough I found Albert Camus. *L'Etranger*.

I should add that my father could not read without running his finger along the line and saying the words out loud very slowly. My mother was very bright but had left school at fourteen. We had no books at home, and anyway I tried not to be at home. I was always in the Pennines, where we lived.

So it is not quite true that I am not a hill walker.

Reading was not so important to my working-class community, unless it was the Bible. Reading the Bible means that you can read anything else – and it makes Shakespeare easy because the language of the King James Version is also the language of Shakespeare. We had a strong oral tradition in the north of England, and people often forget that not being able to read, or not reading, even fifty years ago, let alone a hundred years ago, was very different from not reading now.

We live under 24/7 saturation bombing from an enervated mass media and a bogus manufactured popular culture. If you don't read you will likely be watching telly, or on the computer, or listening to fake music from puppet-show bands.

When the families I knew in my northern textile town didn't read – and they didn't – they were in the brass band, or in the choir, telling their own stories down the pub or on the greyhound track, finding the quiet pleasure of mending kit or working the allotment, or walking for miles in the Pennines. I am not glamorising this working-class life; it was hard and short, and I could not stay there and I would not want it back. But it had a genuine culture of its own – roots up – and it was not force-fed adverts, consumerism and *The X Factor*.

The consequences of homogenised mass culture plus the failure of our education system and our contempt for books and art (it's either entertainment or elitist, never vital and democratic), mean that not reading cuts off the possibility of private thinking, or of a trained mind, or of a sense of self not dependent on external factors.

A trained mind is a mind that can concentrate. Attention Deficit Disorder is not a disease; it is a consequence of not reading. Teach a child to read and keep that child reading and you will change everything. And yes, I mean everything.

Back to the mountain.

Powerfully argued in *The Living Mountain* is the need to be physical, to be in the body, and to let the senses and the soul work in harmony with the mind. This seems a long way from lying in bed and reading a book. But it isn't far at all.

Reading stills the body for a while, allowing rest without torpor and quiet without passivity. Reading is not a passive act. Engaged in the book, in company with the writer, the mind can roam where it will. Such freedom to roam reminds us that body and mind both need exercise and activity, and that neither the mind nor the body can cope with confinement. And if the body has to cope with confinement, then all the more reason to have developed a mind that knows how to roam.

In the last months of her long life Nan Shepherd was in hospital unable to climb her beloved mountains. But her mind went on climbing. She could not be trapped.

Reading is a way through, a way in, a way out. It is a way of life. The rewards are immense.

Nicholas Carr

The Dreams of Readers

Here's a word you don't come across much any more: spermatic. Not only does it feel archaic and arcane, as if it had been extracted from the nether regions of a mouldy physiology handbook, but it seems fatally tainted with political incorrectness. Only the rash or the drunken would dare launch the word into a conversation at a cocktail party. It wasn't always such a pariah. In an essay published a century and a half ago the American poet and philosopher Ralph Waldo Emerson chose the adjective to describe the experience of reading: 'I find certain books vital and spermatic, not leaving the reader what he was.' For Emerson, the best books – the 'true ones' – 'take rank in our life with parents and lovers and passionate experiences, so medicinal, so stringent, so revolutionary, so authoritative'.

Books are not only alive; they give life, or at least give it a new twist.

Emerson drew a distinction between his idea of reading and one expressed a few centuries earlier by Montaigne, who termed books 'a languid pleasure'. Both men, it strikes me, had it right. Like Montaigne, I have spent many happy hours under the spell of books, enchanted by the beauty of the prose, the plot's intrigue or the elegance of the argument. But there have also been times when, like Emerson, I have felt the transforming power of a book, when reading becomes a means not just of diversion or enlightenment, but of regeneration. One closes such a book a different person from the one who opened it. In his poem 'Two Tramps in Mud Time', Robert Frost, one of Emerson's many heirs, wrote of the rare moments in life when 'love and need are one, / And the work is play for mortal stakes'. That seems to me a perfect description of reading at its most vital and spermatic.

My life has been punctuated by books. *The Lord of the Rings* and *The Martian Chronicles* gave shape and heft to my boyhood, opening frontiers to wander in and marvel at far beyond my suburban surroundings. The tumult of my teenage years was fuelled by rock records, but

it was put into perspective by books as various
as Kerouac's *On the Road* and Hemingway's *In
Our Time*, Philip Roth's *Portnoy's Complaint* and
Joseph Heller's *Something Happened*. During my
twenties a succession of thin volumes of verse
– Frost's *A Witness Tree*, Philip Larkin's *Whitsun
Weddings*, Seamus Heaney's *North* – were the
wedges I used to prise open new ways of seeing
and feeling. The list goes on, decade after
decade: Hardy's *Return of the Native*, Joyce's
Ulysses, Cormac McCarthy's *Blood Meridian*, Neil
Sheehan's *A Bright Shining Lie*, Denis Johnson's
Jesus' Son and, recently, the wondrous voyage
that is Patrick O'Brian's Aubrey–Maturin series.
Who would I be without those books? Someone
else.

Psychologists and neurobiologists have begun
studying what goes on in our minds as we read
literature, and what they're discovering lends
scientific weight to Emerson's observation. One
of the trailblazers in this field is Keith Oatley,
a cognitive psychologist at the University
of Toronto and the author of several novels,
including the widely acclaimed *The Case of Emily
V.* 'For a long time,' Oatley recently told the
Canadian magazine *Quill & Quire*, 'we've been
talking about the benefits of reading with respect

to vocabulary, literacy, and these such things. We're now beginning to see that there's a much broader impact.' The source of this broader impact appears to lie in the complex effects that reading a work of literature, particularly narrative literature, has on the human brain. In his 2011 book *Such Stuff as Dreams: The Psychology of Fiction* Oatley explains:

> we don't just respond to fiction (as might
> be implied by the idea of reader response),
> or receive it (as might be implied by
> reception studies), or appreciate it (as in art
> appreciation), or seek its correct
> interpretation (as seems sometimes to be
> suggested by the New Critics). We create
> our own version of the piece of fiction, our
> own dream, our own enactment.

Making sense of what transpires in a book's unreal reality appears to depend on 'making a version of the action ourselves, inwardly'.

One particularly intriguing study, conducted a few years ago by research psychologists at Washington University in St Louis, illuminates Oatley's point. The scholars used brain scans to examine the cellular activity that occurs inside people's heads as they read stories. They found, according to a report on the study, that 'readers mentally simulate each new situation encountered in a narrative'. The groups of nerve cells, or neurons, that are activated in the brains of readers 'closely mirror those involved when [they] perform, imagine, or observe similar real-world activities'. When, for example, a character in a story puts a pencil down on a desk, the neurons that control muscle movements fire in a reader's brain. When a character goes through a door to enter a room, electrical charges begin to flow through the areas in a reader's brain that are involved in spatial representation and navigation. The actions and sensations portrayed in a story are, moreover, woven together 'with personal knowledge from [each reader's] past experiences'. Every reader of a book creates, in Oatley's terms, his own dream of the work – and he inhabits that dream as if it were an actual place.

When we open a book, it seems that we really do enter, as far as our brains are concerned, a new world – one conjured not just out of the author's words, but out of our own memories and desires – and it is our cognitive immersion in that world that gives reading its rich emotional force. Psychologists draw a distinction between two kinds of emotions that can be inspired by a work of art. There are the 'aesthetic emotions' that we feel when we view art from a distance, as a spectator: a sense of beauty or of wonder, for instance, or a feeling of awe at the artist's craft or the work's unity. These are the emotions that Montaigne likely had in mind when he spoke of the languid pleasure of reading. And then there are the 'narrative emotions' that we experience when, through the sympathetic actions of our nervous system, we become part of a story, when the distance between the attendee and the attended evaporates. These are the emotions Emerson may have had in mind when he described the spermatic, life-giving force of a 'true book'.

Readers routinely speak of how books have changed them. A 1999 survey of people who read for pleasure found that nearly two-thirds of them believe they have been transformed in lasting ways by reading. This is no mere fancy. Experiencing strong emotions has been shown to cause alterations in brain functions, and that appears to hold true for the emotions we experience purely through reading. 'The emotions evoked by literary fiction,' reports Oatley in a 2010 paper written with psychologist Raymond

Mar of York University in Toronto, 'have an influence on our cognitive processing after the reading experience has ended.' Although the extent of that influence has yet to be measured in a laboratory, it seems likely that the unusual length of time that we spend immersed in the world of a book would result in particularly strong emotional responses and, in turn, particularly strong cognitive changes. These effects would be further amplified, argues Oatley, by the remarkably 'deep simulation of experience that accompanies our engagement with literary narratives'.

A recent experiment conducted by Oatley and three colleagues suggests that the emotions stirred by literature can even alter, in subtle but real ways, people's personalities. The researchers recruited 166 university students and gave them a standard personality test that measures such traits as extraversion, conscientiousness, and agreeableness. One group of the participants read the Chekhov short story 'The Lady with the Toy Dog,' while a control group read a synopsis of the story's events, stripped of its literary qualities. Both groups then took the personality test again. The results revealed that the people 'who read the short story experienced significantly greater change in personality than the control group', and the effect appeared to be tied to the strong emotional response that the story provoked. What was particularly interesting, Oatley says, is that the readers 'all changed in somewhat different ways'. A book is rewritten in the mind of every reader, and the book rewrites each reader's mind in a unique way, too.

What is it about literary reading that gives it such sway over how we think and feel and perhaps even who we are? Norman Holland, a former scholar at the McKnight Brain Institute at the University of Florida, has been studying literature's psychological effects for many years, and he offers a provocative answer to that question. Although our emotional and intellectual responses to events in literature mirror, at a neuronal level, the responses that we would feel if we actually experienced those events, the mind we read with, argues Holland in his book *Literature and the Brain*, is a very different mind from the one we use to navigate the real world. In our day-to-day lives we are always trying to manipulate or otherwise act on our surroundings, whether it's by turning a car's steering wheel or frying an egg or clicking on a link at a website. But when we open a book our expectations and our attitudes change drastically. Because we understand that 'we cannot or will not change the work of art by our actions', we are relieved of our desire to exert an influence over objects and people and hence are able to 'disengage our [cognitive] systems for initiating actions'. That frees us to become absorbed in the imaginary world of the literary work. We read the author's words with 'poetic faith', to borrow a phrase that the psychologically astute Coleridge used two centuries ago.

'We gain a special trance-like state of mind in which we become unaware of our bodies and our environment,' explains Holland. 'We are "transported".' It is only when we leave behind the incessant busyness of our lives in society that we open ourselves to literature's transformative emotional power. That doesn't mean that reading is antisocial. The central subject of literature is society, and when we lose ourselves in a book we often receive an education in the subtleties and vagaries of human relations. Several studies have shown that reading tends to make us more empathetic, more alert to the inner lives of others. The reader withdraws in order to connect more deeply.

The scientific discoveries about book-reading's

psychological and cognitive effects won't come as a surprise to any lover of literature. But even if the evidence serves mainly to confirm our common sense, it is nevertheless important. It arrives at a crucial moment in the history of literature, when more and more people are choosing to read books on computer screens rather than from pages. As this sudden and possibly epochal shift has gained momentum, a strangely distorted view of reading has gained some cultural currency. A group of Internet enthusiasts has taken to referring to the book, in its traditional form, as a 'passive' medium, lacking the 'interactivity' of websites, apps and video games. Because a page of paper can't accommodate links, 'Like' buttons, search boxes, comment forms and all the other spurs to online activity that we've become accustomed to, the reasoning goes, the readers of books must be mere consumers of content, inert caricatures of Montaigne's languid reader. A prominent publishing consultant, Jeff Jarvis, gave voice to this way of thinking in a post on his blog in 2006. Claiming that printed pages 'create, at best, a one-way relationship with a reader', he concluded that, in the Internet era, 'the book is an outdated means of communicating information'. He declared that 'print is where words go to die'.

Anyone who would reduce a book to 'a means of communicating information', as if it were a canister for shuttling facts and figures among bureaucrats, is probably not the best guide to the possibilities of literary experience. But when foolish ideas move into the slipstream of technological progress, they can travel far – and cause considerable damage. Already the makers of e-reading devices, as well as the publishers of the books that go into them, are embracing the notion that books require a digital upgrade. Books 'often live a vibrant life offline', one Google executive has said, but they will be able to 'live an even more exciting life online'. Although early versions of popular e-readers like the Kindle and the Nook did a pretty good job of replicating the tranquillity of a simple page of text, it now seems likely that the page's calm, and the immersive reading it encourages, will be broken as a book's words are made to compete for a reader's attention with a welter of onscreen tools, messaging systems and other eye-catching diversions. The very form of a book seems fated to change as the written word shifts to a new means of production and distribution.

Not all books are literature, of course. Books of a purely practical nature – manuals, guides and certain types of textbooks, for instance – may well become more useful when their words are supplemented with an array of new features, from embedded videos and soundtracks to cut-and-paste buttons and comment threads. Unfortunately, when new features are added to consumer gadgets, they tend to be applied in a broad and often indiscriminate manner. The cutting edge cuts all ways. Penguin Books recently released, with great fanfare, what it calls an 'amplified edition' of *On the Road*, designed as a downloadable application for Apple's iPad. 'Tricked out with more fancy bells and whistles than a BMW M5', as a *New York Times* reviewer put it, the book app comes with interactive maps, audio snippets, video clips, slideshows and a touchscreen interface. A simple tap on Kerouac's words whisks the reader out of the story and into the digital marginalia. I'm sure I would have enjoyed playing with the *On the Road* app when I was a kid, but I doubt it would have rattled my soul in the way my tattered paperback did.

'The house was quiet and the world was calm. / The reader became the book.' So begins a haunting Wallace Stevens poem about the uncanniness of reading, published in the 1947 collection *Transport to Summer*. Norman Holland's observation that the deepest kinds of reading require a dampening of our urge to act, a withdrawal from quotidian busyness, is really just a variation on Stevens' theme. What both poet and scientist tell us is that Montaigne's and Emerson's views may actually be more in concert than in conflict. It may be that a reader has to enter a state of languid pleasure before he can experience the full spermatic vitality of a book. Far from being a sign of passivity, the reader's outward repose sets the stage for the most profound kind of inner activity.

One thing I've noticed about myself and other devoted readers – and I think it's revealing – is that we often have a hard time separating a book's words from the paper the words are printed on. Our love of reading manifests itself in a romantic attachment to the physical book. A volume on a shelf becomes a kind of sacred relic. Glancing at its spine spurs memories of the time in which it was read or of the emotions it aroused. Some readers even rhapsodise, Proust-like, about the way books smell. They relish the ink-and-adhesives scent of a freshly printed book and the musty aroma of an old one. I confess that I've never shared that particular passion. A fragrant book simply makes me sneeze. My own attachment is more to the heft of a printed volume. When I hold a book in my hands, I feel as though I'm holding a metaphor for its contents. One journeys through a book, going deeper with each turn of a page, as one journeys through a story. My copy of *Moby-Dick*, that most spermatic of novels, is a pliable brick: 800 pages of small, tightly spaced type. It tells me to pack a trunk, to steel myself for a long and hazardous journey.

There are those who dismiss the reverence readers feel for physical books as mere sentimentality. Words are words, they say, however they're presented. I'm not so sure. Back in the seventh century, when books were still handwritten by scribes, the theologian Isaac of Nineveh wrote of how it felt to make his way through a long series of pages: 'as in a dream, I enter a state when my sense and thoughts are concentrated. Then, with the prolonging of this silence the turmoil of memories is stilled in my heart, ceaseless waves of joy are sent me by inner thoughts, beyond expectation suddenly arising to delight my heart.' Reading is more than the visual decoding of alphabetic symbols. It is a state of mind, a dream of life, and a book, if it is going to be a true book, needs to be more than a container of words; it needs to be a shield against busyness, a transport to elsewhere. Stevens put it simply: 'The house was quiet because it had to be.'

Dr Maryanne Wolf
and Dr Mirit Barzillai

Questions for a Reader

Reading transforms the human brain, which transforms the mind, which transforms the life of every reader.

Few of us ever stop to realise how momentous and semi-miraculous the achievement of reading is for our species. We were never born to read or write anything. Unlike vision or language, reading has no genetic programme that unfolds to create an ideal form of itself. Rather, learning to read lies outside the original repertoire of the human brain's functions and requires a whole new circuit to be built afresh with each new reader.

Literally and physiologically, the brain changes itself by building a versatile 'reading circuit' out of a rearrangement of its original structures, such as visual, conceptual and language areas. Which structures are recruited, and how extensively and deeply they are used, depends on many factors. More specifically, because there is no genetic blueprint for reading, the brain's reading circuit will adapt itself to what is being asked – by the characteristics of the writing system (e.g. English alphabet vs Hebrew alphabet vs Chinese logo-syllabary); by the formation process (how much, how well the child is taught to use all the many cognitive resources available to each part of the process); by the content of what is read; and finally by the medium (e.g. sign, book, Internet, e-book). This means that the very plasticity that allows every novice reader to build a fresh new circuit to read could prove to be not only a gift, but also an Achilles heel.

The specific factors that affect the formation of the reading circuits take on special significance in the present moment, as we move from a literacy-based culture to one dominated by digital tools and a digital sense of time. Immersed and shaped anew by varied technological mediums, the reading brain as we know it will be changed and to some degree supplanted by a different reading circuit. No one fully knows what form this new circuit will take or what this will ultimately mean for all of us.

What we do know is that for centuries our

species has honed the present 'expert' reading brain. We have done so by learning over time to integrate decoding skills with what we refer to as the 'deep-reading' processes: e.g. analogical thought, inferential reasoning, perspective-taking, critical analysis, imagination, insight, novel thought, etc. The integration of these processes during reading is automatic for expert readers, but it can never be taken for granted. Rather, how well deep-reading processes are incorporated in the reading act depends significantly on how that circuit was formed over years of learning. The expert reader must expend considerable cognitive effort and time (in milliseconds and in years) to reach the point where the reading act leads automatically to the expansion of personal thought.

A pivotal question in today's historical transition is whether the more time-consuming demands of these deep-reading processes will atrophy or, in fact, never be fully formed in children raised within a culture whose principal mediums for reading increasingly advantage speed, multitasking and the processing of the next 'new' piece of information. Will an immersion in digitally dominated forms of reading change the capacity and the motivation of the reader (expert and novice) to utilise their more sophisticated reading capacities, encouraging them to think deeply, reflectively and in an intellectually autonomous manner? Will new readers feel such efforts warrant no justification, since the analyses of many others are simply a click away? Or will easy access to sophisticated analyses and potential collaborators serve to enrich and motivate further thought and discussion, bringing students to new levels of discovery? Will the presence of digital tools such as translations and definitions serve to enhance the reading experience, by acting as bootstraps when difficulties are encountered, or will they disrupt it? What will such directions mean to the intellectual autonomy of individuals?

These questions cannot be answered yet by existing evidence, but there are important insights from the history of literacy, neuroscience and literature that can help better prepare us to ask critical questions now – that is, before the reading brains of the next generation are fully altered. The Greek transition from an oral culture to a literacy-based culture provides a valuable analogue to our present transition. Perhaps somewhat ironically, Socrates, Greece's most eloquent apologist for an oral culture, protested at the acquisition of literacy on the basis of concerns that are as prescient today as they remain surprising. Socrates argued that the seeming permanence of the printed word would delude the young into thinking they had accessed the essence of some aspect of knowledge, rather than simply decoded it. For him only the intellectually effortful process of probing, analysing and internalising knowledge would enable the young to develop a lifelong, personal approach to knowing and thinking, which could lead them to their ultimate goals – wisdom and virtue. Only the examined word and the 'examined life' were worth pursuing, with all the intellectual discipline and exertion they required. Literacy, Socrates believed, would short-circuit both.

Steeped in oral culture, it was difficult for Socrates to imagine that the printed word would give rise to a complex reading brain that would foster the development of an internalised platform for probing, analysing and reflecting on what is read. That said, there was a trade-off made then, with aspects of oral culture and memory lost for ever – just as there will be a trade-off in our present transition. Unlike then, we can examine with far more knowledge both what we have in the present reading brain and what we hope to preserve. A brief summary of the first 500 milliseconds of the reading act illumines the existing panoply of components that come together when we read. As we read even a single word, the first milliseconds of reading are devoted to the activation of extensive areas of the cortex and subcortical regions that are necessary for 'decoding' the word's visual information and connecting it to all that we know about the word. This latter knowledge requires input from regions responsible for everything from the word's sounds to its many possible meanings and associations, to its varied grammatical and pragmatic functions. Over time, this first, large set of operations becomes virtually automatic, thereby allowing us in the next milliseconds to go beyond the decoded text. Within the next pivotal milliseconds we enter a cognitive space where we can connect the decoded information to all that we know and feel. It is within the latter phase of the expert reading circuit that we learn to connect the decoded information to the 'deep-reading' processes, and ultimately to our capacity to think new thoughts. This is the generative, cognitively transformative platform at the heart of the reading process. It is unique in the intellectual history of the species.

Perhaps no one better captured what and how the reader begins to think in those last milliseconds of the reading circuit than the French novelist Marcel Proust. He characterised this 'heart of reading' as that moment when 'that which is the end of their [the author's] wisdom is but the beginning of ours' (Proust, 1906). Insights from Proust, Socrates and cognitive neuroscience research converge here. However we define it, Proust's 'wisdom' represents the acme within the expert reading brain's circuit that is, itself, the sum of multiple, personal, deep-reading capacities. Proust's wisdom and the reading brain's internal platform for thought are the basis for Socrates' wisdom, which is the basis for the 'examined' life. Through the internalised development of all these capacities, human beings learn to think in new ways. As former editor Peter Dimock writes (2010), 'this kind of reading, then, is a time of internal solitary consciousness in which the reading consciousness is brought up to the level of the knowledge of the author – *the farthest point another mind has reached*, as it were' (our italics).

The problem is that there is neither genetic guarantee nor cultural pressure to ensure that the individual novice reader will ever reach such an intellectual 'farthest point' as described by Dimock, or form the expert reading-brain circuitry necessary to attain it. As demonstrated in existing research, the reading circuit in its current iteration can be fully fashioned and fully implemented over time, or it can be 'short-circuited' at any juncture in its development: e.g. early on in its formation period – through poor instruction, impoverished environments or inadequate motivation and opportunity; or after its formation, in the diminished execution of all its available cognitive resources under certain conditions. Several key questions emerge at the present moment: will short-circuiting occur based on the medium used for most reading before the reading circuit is fully formed? Will the short-circuiting of some processes be replaced by the addition of a whole new repertoire of cognitive skills better suited to the pace and glut of information available today? What are the intellectual advantages and costs involved in the different possible scenarios?

For example, will the omnipresence of innumerable distractions for attention, coupled with the sheer volume of information available, contribute in our young to a mindset *towards* reading that seeks to reduce the massive information to its lowest conceptual denominator as quickly as possible? With too much before them to grasp, and a set towards immediate feedback, will today's novice reader learn to want things simple, quick and explained by others? Alternatively, will young people immersed in technological innovation become adept at prioritising, sorting and critically evaluating information, adapting different types of reading styles based upon their purpose (finding info, understanding it)? The opportunities to engage with all manner of subjects and audiences might fuel their motivation to read and communicate, sparking new thoughts and ideas. Will the flexibility of digital text (alterations in size, access to definitions, etc.) actually enhance the reading experience for many readers, propelling them into a deeper engagement with text, or will such enhancements serve as further distractions?

There are no pat answers and no binary solutions for any of these questions. Technological innovation is critical to all of us if we are to advance. Few need to be reminded of the life-changing advantages of the digital culture's technological advances. It is clear that today's children, not tomorrow's, require a new set of intellectual tools and capacities if they are to become productive members of their culture. But as a society, we need to understand how our collective immersion in daunting amounts of digital information has the potential to either encourage intellectual exploration and creation or to 'damp down' readers' use of their most cognitively demanding resources by encouraging speed and sound-bites. We need to know the implications of a dependency on external platforms of knowledge for the depth and autonomy of our thought.

Ultimately, we may already have within our grasp the tools to conceptualise what the 'new readers' of the twenty-first century need: a differently evolving reading circuit, one that connects the existing expert deep-reading skills to the evolving information-processing skills in order to be able to use the resources of the twenty-first-century external platforms of knowledge wisely and well. The task is to figure out how to get there. We will need many minds to plot this progression.

Just as in the Greeks' transition from oral to literacy-based cultures, our issues today are not about whether we are to become a digital culture or not. Socrates' concerns were never really about whether the Greek youth should read or not. Socrates worried that a lack of internalised knowledge would lead to a lack of reflection about one's personal relationship to the acme of knowledge, wisdom and virtue. So too now. In this historical transition we must focus on the essential questions about the reciprocal relation between the quality of reading – at every stage of its development – and the quality of thought and virtue in individuals and in society. Will alterations in how we read over time change how we think? And, finally, will changes in how we think alter the quality of how we live out our lives? No one has the answers to these questions, but in asking we begin their investigation and recognise their importance for the intellectual, social and ethical development of our species.

www.vintage-books.co.uk